Escape From Mexico

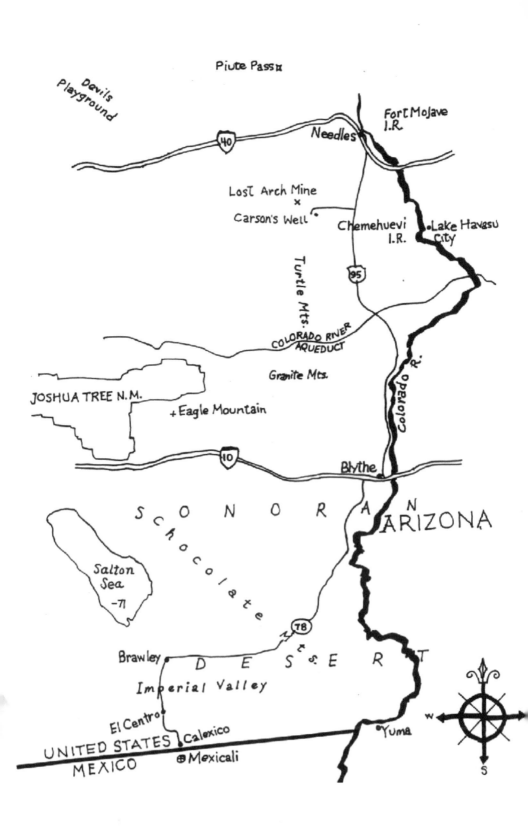

Escape From Mexico

❉

Lewis Horton

For information contact:
Creative Arts Book Company
833 Bancroft Way
Berkeley, California 94710
1-800-848-7789

ISBN 088739-329-2
Library of Congress Catalog Number 99-69768

Printed in the United States of America

To My Father

Escape From Mexico

"All that we know who lie in (jail)
Is that the wall is strong;
And that each day is like a year,
A year whose days are long."

—O. Wilde

PREAMBLE

I mentioned to the tank boss that I'd been asking guards to let me make a phone call to the American Embassy since being arrested a week ago. The boss said he'd see what he could do. At roll call a guard took me in the office, dialed the American Consul in Calexico, and handed me the phone.

A secretary answered.

"I'm an American citizen," I said. "This is an emergency. I need to speak to the American Consul."

After a pause, a man said, "Hello."

"I'm an American citizen; a soldier in the United States Army. I'm being held in the federal prison at Mexicali."

"Yes, I know all that," the man said. "What do you want me to do?"

"Well, if you know, then do something to get me out."

"What for?" he said. "You're guilty, aren't you?"

"No, I'm not guilty! Why do you say that? You haven't even talked to me."

"I'll look into it," he said, and hung up.

So began and ended my contact with the United States Government; with all its branches, departments, bureaus, offices, humane outreach social workers, support groups, including the United States Army in which I was a soldier in good standing with a valid weekend pass in my wallet.

The path to the Mexicali federal prison hadn't been straight down, some of it had been sideways. How had I come to be in such a miserable state? How many orphans had I whacked out with my Uzi? What mayhem had I wreaked in the crowded senior center with my fuel-injected chainsaw?

ESCAPE FROM MEXICO

On a cold day in March we soldiers were happy to be departing the snows of Fort Leonard Wood, Missouri. War games were being staged in sunny Southern California. We were practicing for a war in Southeast Asia, so, naturally, we were sent to the Mojave Desert. At the end of the exercise the real body count stood at forty-seven confirmed dead, killed one way or another.

On a map of the United States the Mojave seems to be right outside Los Angeles. So it appeared to guys in the company, most of whom were from the south and mid west. I was from northern California, but I had the same misconception. Even Mexico didn't seem far away. The nearest military base was at Long Beach Harbor. Sailors, too weakened by syphilis to ship out, would be our only competition for available ladies. So we chose to think.

One GI asked me how far Graumann's Theater was from Mojave. His mother wanted a Chinese lantern. I told him I didn't know, but I'd probably pick up a coolie hat when we got there. Guys figured the Mojave was like a theme park with elephant trains leaving for the city every few minutes. I was ready to believe it.

The Army showed two training films before we departed. The first movie was about rotting gums. I don't know how they got the camera inside the patient's mouth and still had room for lighting. If my camera had been used, even covered with a rubber glove, I would've thrown the thing away afterward.

In the second film, *Dos and Don'ts in the Desert*, a soldier sitting in a tent drinks a quart of whiskey. He takes off his shirt and cap, wanders into the desert, and passes out. Fortunately, a couple of GIs happen by and rescue their comrade. One of the rescuers looked like Ronald Reagan.

At the Fort Leonard Wood airstrip, fatigue-clad, combat ready, our company climbed aboard a DC something or other with four motors. Painted on at least one side of the aircraft was the identification: Trans-Intercontinental Flight Services, Inc. A couple of years later this same plane crashed and killed all the soldiers on board.

No one could remember having seen anything larger than a Piper Cub take off from the airstrip. But if the four-motor plane had landed, unless it was towed there, we agreed it should be able to take off.

The stewardess on board the plane, the only woman, gave us sticks of chewing gum, then she sat up front and chatted with one of the pilots for most of the five-hour flight. Once we were airborne I got the worst earache of my life. I pressed the palm of my hand over the aching ear canal and the pain lessened.

From Fort Leonard Wood, a sprawling facility beside Route 66 in Missouri, we flew to an airstrip by Route 66 in the Mojave Desert. Knowing we were following the highway across country gave me confidence in our safe arrival. As soon as we landed, my earache stopped. The weather was sunny and windy, very windy. There was nothing in any direction but scruffy desert ringed by distant mountains. We collected our duffel bags, climbed into the back of trucks, and off we went—down or up Route 66.

2

No one asked directions to Graumann's Chinese Theater. The only question was "Where in the hell is the nearest town?" That would be Needles, California, ten miles from our desert camp as the turkey vulture flies. They don't fly as much as they glide around in circles. Mostly, they walk along the highway eating road-kill.

Our trucks pulled off the road and stopped at our temporary home in the desert. Except for wooden floors nailed together by an engineer company, there was nothing but piles of materials: canvas, ropes, poles, fasteners—all the stuff we'd need to erect our eight man tents. Weeks later, as I lay sweltering in my tent, listening to seven other guys snore, fart, and belch, I wondered why the Army was so good to us. Why did they provide us with wooden floors? Why not just let us use the God-given desert for a floor? One night when I was thinking about something else, the answer came to me. Tents pitched right on the sandy, rotten soil would have fallen down.

We set to work setting up our tents, a task made difficult by fierce winds blowing eyes and canvas full of dirt. Communication from more than three feet away was all but impossible.

At our tent site I held one end of a rope attached to a pile of canvas. Poles were assembled, fasteners driven into the platform, and wood frame sidings added to the floors. When our tent rose, my rope was fastened to one end of the top. It took an hour or more.

What we needed was always in a crate that hadn't been unpacked yet. It was getting dark when we finished. We hadn't even started on the big mess tent. Back in the trucks we went for a trip to the engineers' mess hall.

At the engineers' company area we reluctantly climbed out of our trucks into a howling wind that drove sand like a paint stripper. The mess hall was a wooden building with lights. General Patton had used the facility for his troops while training for *tanko a tanko* combat with General Rommel.

Environmentalists would treat us as harshly as Patton for screwing up the desert.

> In two weeks of May 1964, 89,000 Army troops fanned out over the desert west of Needles in something called Operation Desert Strike—a training exercise that laid environmental waste to sizable swaths of the east Mojave. The groundwork (so to speak) for such activity had been established during World War II at the so-called Desert Training Center, an area comprising some 17,500 square miles in Southern California, Arizona, and Nevada—'the largest and best training ground in the United States,' according to its commanding general, George S. Patton.

A specific indictment of our swath wasting:

> General George Patton's Desert Training Center, in the early years of World War II, and Operation Desert Strike—a massive army ground exercise that took place in the eastern Mojave in the spring of 1964—were both known to have decimated local Gopherus agassizii populations.

The casual reader probably thinks, as I did at first, that the Gopherus agassizii is a gopher. But, no, it's a desert tortoise. What I wouldn't give for a swath-wasted tortoise steak, medium-well, smothered in mushrooms. Not counting the chewing gum we'd been given on the airplane, it had been twelve hours since we ate.

The engineers company cook had whipped up a pasta dish—noodles over which a thin red gruel had been poured. Absent were all the little tasty specks and flecks that make food worth tasting: oregano, thyme, rosemary, basil, sage, parsley flakes, pepper. I couldn't even taste garlic. It was to spaghetti what the military is to real life.

I thought of my pilgrimages to New Joe's, Old Joe's, Original Joe's, Broadway Joe's, Sonoma Joe's, Vanessi's. In those days I was becoming a spaghetti connoisseur. Late one night at New Joe's on Broadway in San Francisco I was sitting at the end of the counter near the door. I was ravishing a plate of half spaghetti and half ravioli, with a side order of garlic bread. Suddenly, onto the stool next to me hopped what looked like a small red bear, or huge furry marmot. Startled, I turned to see what it was. I think I said, "Whoa!" It was Carol Doda, a small gorgeous lady with large endowments. She was an early version of Dolly Parton, only built better. Ms. Doda wore a red fur coat and nothing else I could see, except for high heeled shoes. She was grabbing a bite to eat between shows at the Condor Club on the corner of Broadway and Columbus where Carol was the star attraction of an act headlined: "TOPLESS . . . NIGHTLY." Her curvaceous outline in neon tubes filled a huge marquee dominating the intersection. She ordered half a baked chicken.

I don't know who sat next to me in the engineers mess hall. I was too busy wolfing down noodles. Regrettably, there were no seconds. Back outside General Patton's place, the wind was gale force. Anything not swirling in your face—dirt, sand, hot dog wrappers—was blown clear away. Visibility was nearly zero. We somehow found the trucks, then the highway, and returned to tent city.

A generator had been set up next to headquarters tent. It powered a string of lights down the main path between the other tents. As we drove into the company area, the bulbs sputtered and went out for the rest of the night. We found our tents by flashlight. Inside, I sat on my cot in the dark, my sleeping bag still rolled up. Nobody got undressed. The wind outside was fierce and the weight of me and seven other guys was holding the wood floor onto the desert. The canvas tent and wood frames fastened to it were being ripped from their foundation.

One side of our tent tore completely loose and rose, flapping in the cyclone. We exited through the new opening as sand and dirt blasted in. Standing in the desert, peeking through cracks in our fingers, we watched as tent and frames blew away. Next morning we found our tent wrapped around a cactus, ropes still attached.

In some tents, guys tried to be heroes and hold the sides down as the wind tore them loose. Like cheap cigar fillings, wrapped in canvas, the heroes were blown into the desert. Their shouts and cries helped us locate them. I don't know what happened next because I crawled in the back of a truck and, using my arm for a pillow, fell asleep. Next day I was told, after the wind blew everything down, it swirled once or twice about camp and conked out.

3

In the morning our tent was found and unwrapped from a cactus. It was time for breakfast. The cooks hadn't gotten the stoves together so we had cold white bread with syrup on top, French toast, almost. Fortunately, there were seconds and thirds. After breakfast, we nailed the frames back together, and put the canvas back up. For lunch we had bologna sandwiches. Even though the wind had calmed down, there was sand in everything. Chewing on the bologna was like eating cheap clams.

The afternoon went by slowly as we erected the mess tent. For supper we had hamburgers. The meat was cooked, the buns toasty. We filled our metal trays with hot pork and beans, salad, and canned peaches. I thought I'd died and gone to Sweden to be with the draft-dodging offspring of rich people. That night we slept in our tents in sleeping bags on cots. A light was strung in each tent. I was asleep before the light was turned off.

The wind never blew again during Desert Strike like it did that first day and night. Maybe it had never blown that hard before in the history of the Mojave. Who knew? There was nowhere to buy a newspaper. No TV or radio, except for a hillbilly station in Arizona.

The Army, as a source of information, is useless. Would you rather be ignorant of facts, or filled with miserable lies? In the Army you can do both. If the hurricane winds we'd just experienced had been turbulence caused by a comet about to destroy planet earth, the Army would be busy drafting guidelines on alternate sources of Brasso for belt buckle maintenance.

Back in Fort Leonard Wood, hanging on the wall of our company headquarters, were two examples of military intelligence at work. An iron triangle and striking bar, painted red, were mounted on the wall above a sign, "SOUND ALARM IN CASE OF FIRE." Next to this emergency warning system hung a triangle and a striking bar painted yellow. The second sign read, "SOUND ALARM IN CASE OF NUCLEAR ATTACK." Either of these advanced systems could have been brought with us to the desert to tell us when it was time to eat.

Life in the desert soon settled into a routine. First thing in the morning I'd shake out my boots. It was the only bit of advice from the training films I followed. While Ronald Reagan drank a quart of whiskey and ran into the desert without a hat, his sensible tent mate, Jack Elam, held his pair of boots upside down and knocked them together. Two scorpions, several deadly millipedes, and a coral snake fell out.

Actually, sand in our food was more aggravating than scorpions. Pots and pans attract blowing dirt. After cookware is cleaned and dried, sand gets back on them before it can be put away. Even sergeants complained about grit in their food. I realized it was an act of God and not an Army plot.

4

I never saw a scorpion, but I did see a coral snake. A guy killed one outside his tent with an entrenching tool. He scooped the small snake onto his shovel and chased a guy from New York around camp, trying to throw the serpent on his head. The New Yorker hated bugs of all kinds, including snakes, so he ran for his life. It was a sensible move; he didn't know it was dead. One of our desert troop died from a coral snake bite. The bugger had crawled into his sleeping bag.

Roll call was before dawn. We fell out and lined up in the desert. All that purple mountains majesty stuff was drowned out by 220 men farting and belching. You may wonder how a person who just woke up with an empty stomach can belch. I was curious, myself. It's an old Midwestern kind of humor raised to an art form in Minnesota and Iowa. Whenever it gets too quiet, the prankster sucks air into his large intestine and using diaphragmatic manipulation produces tremendous belches. It sounds like the belchee's throat is rupturing.

Digestive tracts competed with complaints about the desert, the weather, food, tents, sand, pay, and sergeants. We were not happy campers. We were living a National Geographic special with a Beavis and

Butthead soundtrack. I was present during dawn but, unlike the soldiers in Hamlet, never witnessed "the morning in russet mantle clad walking o'er the dew on yon high eastern hill."

After breakfast, instead of physical training, we picked up rocks. Once nets arrived we played volleyball, but for the first week it was just the rocks. Fanning out in single file, we combed the desert between tent city and our ninety trucks parked in a straight row across the wasteland. At first, we picked up any rock bigger than a baseball; then a golf ball, a marble, a BB. When the nets and volleyballs arrived, only fine dirt remained in our area of the Mojave.

We made two rock collecting passes, then it was off to the motor pool a hundred yards away. Our trucks were two and one half ton models called deuce and a halfs. Mine was made in 1949. The cab held two people: the driver and a guy riding shotgun, called the tailgate driver. His job was to open and close the tailgate, making sure the driver didn't back over anyone. A canvas, supported by wooden spars, covered the back, into which fourteen guys could be crammed uncomfortably. Every war movie since WWI has relied heavily on the deuce and a half. It's the truck that hauled Telly Savalas, Charles Bronson, James Coburn, Jim Brown, Clint Walker, Richard Jaeckel, and Steve McQueen.

On ration breakdown, side benches were folded up and the truck held crates of food. Our company delivered much of the food stuffs to mess halls that kept 89,000 soldiers wandering about the Mojave in tanks, trucks, jeeps, and on foot. It's the truck that helped make the world safe from Gopherus agassizii.

The rest of the morning was spent pulling motor stables. Our sergeant said, "By the numbers: raise hood!"

We'd raise our hoods.

"Check oil!"

We'd check the oil.

"Check gas . . . battery, belts, spark plugs, wipers, headlights, tire pressure, canvas, ropes . . ."

You had to always appear busy. An hour could be spent re-tying a rope connected from the canvas to an eyelet on the truck body. Meanwhile, a conversation would develop with the guy on the next truck who was re-tying one of his ropes. Soon it was lunchtime. Or, as they say in the Army, dinner.

After lunch it was back to the motor pool for more work. A guy might untie all his ropes and remove the canvas for sweeping. Or he could rotate a couple of tires. It was unlikely that he'd perform these activities because they were hard work. More likely, he'd go get some grease to lubricate something. Or check out a broom to sweep pieces of broccoli from the back of his truck. Or use a tiny wire brush to clean the battery posts.

Grease, brooms, wire brushes, and minor parts were maintained in a tent by the wrecker. There was always a long line. Tiny wire brushes seemed to go first. Guys weren't upset about standing in line; their idle-ness was enlivened by talking to each other. Trips to the parts tent were interrupted by visits to friends along the way. Stop, chat, maybe help someone re-tie a rope.

Basic training platoon. All Eskimo squad: third row. Includes oldest man (47) to take basic at Fort Ord, and the shortest guy: four feet something. Short guy appears briefly in the movie *Soldier In The Rain*.

5

In a truck convoy the last vehicle is the wrecker. It's supposed to be driven by a mechanic who can repair any breakdown. Our wrecker was driven by a drunken, lunatic dirtbag named Yandell. He'd pumped gas in a Texaco station. When he joined the Army, he called himself a master mechanic. Anyone watching him cross-thread the cap on his Thunderbird wine bottle would realize he wasn't mechanically inclined. Most of the time he'd just smash the cap on with the palm of his hand.

Yandell was big and filthy, covered in grease, dirt, whatever stuck to his uniform. His hands were always grimy. He didn't seem to mind crawling around under trucks. That must be what endeared him to the Army. Of all the rotten luck in the world, he was assigned to our tent. He was also the only guy with a portable radio.

Okie music blasted from our tent when Yandell was in. He took the radio with him when he went out. He'd located a hillbilly station in Arizona and listened to it twenty-four hours a day. I thought Glen Campbell sang Okie music, but this station never played Glen Campbell. It played some kind of aboriginal hillbilly rap. The only names I recognized were Flatt and Scruggs, who I had thought were a team of magicians on the "Ed Sullivan Show."

I asked Yandell once to turn the radio down. As he continued staring blankly at the ceiling of the tent, he said, "Ah caint hear ya. Mah radio's too loud."

At night he'd get in the wrecker and cruise Route 66 looking for a bar or liquor store. Climbing out of the truck, he must have resembled the Creature from the Black Lagoon. When he ran out of money, or Army parts to sell for booze, he'd sit on his bunk in the tent and take deep breaths from a bag containing gas-soaked rags.

After Yandell passed out, we'd turn the radio off to get some sleep. As he lay snoring, covered in dirt and petroleum products, filling the tent with gas fumes, I'd fantasize about adjusting my zippo lighter's flame to its highest point and tossing the mini-blowtorch onto Yandell. I couldn't be sure the conflagration would finish him; even asleep he looked ineradicable. There was a feeling I had that, if I couldn't kill him completely, why bother? Chopping off part of him with an entrenching tool would just result in the part growing back.

Late Friday afternoon, back from the motor pool, we were all waiting to get in the mess tent for supper. A gassed Yandell got into a scuffle with the company clerk who was also drunk. Our entire drinking water supply, a large canvas bag, hung from a wooden tripod outside the mess tent. Yandell picked up the company clerk and shoved him head first into the water bag. Unfortunately, the clerk, who could do to military reports what Yandell did to wine bottle tops, was pulled from the water bag before he drowned. This incident was witnessed by most of the sergeants and officers. Nobody did anything besides rescue the clerk.

One day Yandell drove off in the wrecker, never to return to our tent. The military police found him. He was court-martialed and securely locked away at Leavenworth, Kansas, where I'll bet he didn't have a radio. Even the most brilliant criminal mind can suffer from a slight defect. Yandell's was alcohol and gasoline. Here's what occurred.

Our transportation company staged a training exercise. We were to drive our trucks to different locations around the area. The trucks were old and in poor condition. Except for re-tied ropes and clean battery posts, maintenance had been deferred. All along the highway trucks were broken down. The wrecker was supposed to repair breakdowns but it was nowhere around. Police were called.

The wrecker was found parked outside a bar. Inside, drunker than a skunk, sat Yandell. He'd been there most of the day and was negotiating the sale of the company's last batteries and spark plugs. Once Yandell was safely behind bars, our company commander threw the book at him. When MPs came to our tent to get his stuff, we made sure they took the radio. The motor pool was depleted of parts and we were depleted of Yandell. A fair trade.

It became quieter and more desert-like. Time was reduced to two plodding parts: day and night. Daytime had three things going on: eating, standing in line for tiny brushes, and getting mail. At night we stood in line for beer.

6

After we'd camped a week in the desert, a truck towing a small mobile home parked off the highway between our company area and the engineers down the road. In the evening the trailer opened for business. From one window they sold sandwiches, chips, candy, and sodas. The other window sold beer, two per customer. We'd buy two beers and get back in line. A guy's place in the long line would be saved while he went behind the trailer to take a piss. The beer window was supposed to close at 9 p.m., but they always ran out of beer first.

We were usually standing in the beer line when the sun set on our—moonscape comes to mind. We watched the sun set behind the craters of the moon. I don't know about the rest of the Mojave, but the eastern part isn't like movie deserts, no sparkling white sand, no sand dunes. It's rough ground, small gullies, rocks, dirt, lizards, and scraggly weeds of the tumbling and non-tumbling variety.

One Sunday, my fourth anniversary to be exact, I'd been in the Army four months, me and another guy, Williams, hiked a mile or so from camp to the Colorado River. Our plan was to ride air mattresses down the current. When we reached a town, we'd get off and hitchhike back. Luckily, we forgot to take the mattresses.

Nothing indicated we were nearing the river. We didn't see palm trees, elephant grass, or tall bamboo groves. Suddenly the river was there and it was moving fast. We sat near the bank, cans of beer saved up during the week were put in a notch carved out by the river. We put stones around the beer to protect it from the current.

Taking off my boots and socks, I waded in the river to cool off. As I got to the edge, the bank fell away. There wasn't a gradual slope from ankle to calf to knee to thigh; I was in the river up to my waist. The river bed was loose, shifting gravel. The current was powerful, trying to drag me away. I dove for the bank, catching hold of a thick root. Pulling myself from the river, I realized I hadn't even had time to yell.

Williams sat calmly drinking beer. "That was quick," he said.

"It doesn't take me very long to figure out a river," I said, opening a hot one.

I sat well removed from the river's edge and drank my hot beer. There was nothing to lean against, and no shade. The sun was directly overhead, scorching. Flowers and animals (other than lizards) had been blasted away. Only two stupid humans and a thin patch of weeds remained under the fierce sun. I tried to remember a more miserable time. It didn't take long. The time I was in the Cub Scouts.

7

In the dead of winter my Cub Scout pack decided to go to Twain-Harte in the Sierras for a weekend tobogganing-campout. Snow was piled deep and still falling as we pitched tents. It was too late to cook anything so we ate sandwiches made that morning, washed down with a carton of cold milk. My father, one of the adult volunteers, had used our pickup truck to haul much of the camping gear and toboggans.

A kerosene lamp hanging in our tent provided little light and no heat. Pa and I shared the tent with the scoutmaster and his two sons. The boys commented on the horrible stench coming from the lantern. Their dad told them to stop complaining; it was our only source of heat. When they said they were freezing, he said it was good training. This was nothing. "Just wait until you get to the Boy Scouts." I could wait.

Inside my Arctic sleeping bag, designed by Edmund Hillary or Hopalong Cassidy, I wore every piece of clothing I'd brought with me, including a watch cap and boots. I was freezing. My teeth were chattering so badly I couldn't talk straight. When I clamped my jaws shut, I could hear everybody else's teeth chattering.

After a couple of hours my father rose fully clothed from his sleeping bag and tapped me on the shoulder, signalling me to follow him. In the dark, Pa found his way through the trees to the parking lot. We climbed in the truck cab; he started the engine. While the motor idled, he turned the heater on full blast. The first shot of cold air was warmer than whatever was inside the tent. Soon, hot air filled the cab. All the windows were fogged up like a Turkish bath.

"Is this what it's like to be in Hawaii?" I asked.

"I don't know," he said. "I've never been there."

Pa estimated how much gas we'd need to get back to civilization. When the gas gauge reached that point, he turned off the engine and we returned to camp.

Williams and I finished the last of the red hot beer and threw the empties in the Colorado River. We headed back to camp. Trudging across the desert, I was reminded of a scene from my favorite war movie, *The Bridge on the River Kwai*. After slogging a hundred miles through desert, swamp, and jungle, the devastated prisoners are lined up before Colonel Saito. At the end of his speech, Saito says, "Be happy in your work." If I'd played the character Alec Guiness played, I might've added, "That's easy for you to say."

8

Wednesday afternoon was our squad's day at the laundromat. We loaded our dirty clothes into laundry bags and piled into the back of a couple of trucks. We motored down Route 66 to the town of Needles in San Bernardino County. Outside the laundromat, news racks were filled with Chamber of Commerce literature and real estate books packed with interesting historical stuff.

For example, I guessed that Needles was named for Euphrates P. Needles, the area's first settler who invented the knitting needle. Later he built a factory that pounded out the pointy instruments almost as fast as Hershey, Pennsylvania produces chocolate. My guess was wrong.

Actually, the Needles Post Office and rail station of the Atlantic and Pacific Railroad (now the Santa Fe) were established on February 18, 1883, on the Arizona side of the Colorado River and named after the nearby pinnacles. On October 11 of the same year, the railroad transferred the name to a new town on the California side, a location which was considered better. The name was originally applied to the peaks by the Pacific Railroad Survey, and in whose reports they are frequently mentioned. A map of 1854 labels the peaks in Indian, Asientic Habi, and English, The Needles.

But, why Needles? (Think of used syringes). Why not Pinnacles? How about Asientic Habi? That sounds like old money or a golf course. If Palm Springs had been able to keep its original name, Agua Caliente, it too might have amounted to something. Alas, another town in Sonoma County, had already glommed onto the moniker.

Next to the laundromat was a bar. Two guys in our squad were religious fanatics and didn't drink. We promised the teetotalers some free sodas if they'd watch the laundry bounce around in the machines. A special place in heaven, smoke-free, booze-free, should be set aside for guys like these.

The bartender appeared glad to see us, ten thirsty GIs. A sun-fried, old geezer sipping a draft was the only other person in the bar. He soon left. The beer there was potent, more powerful than the bilge sold at the beer trailer. It confirmed my worst suspicion: the Army was watering our beer. What else were they watering? It was common knowledge they put saltpeter in our food. I hadn't had much lead in my pencil since being drafted. The ladies of Needles, if there were any, could relax.

The tavern had a bar top made from a massive piece of redwood. According to the barkeep, the top was shipped over from L.A. after the original dive burned to the ground. If the counter top had as many coats of Varithene then as it did now, it would have burst spontaneously into flames. The varnish highlighted the wood's grain, making beautiful swirls and patterns. Brass spittoons and a brass foot rail added to the Western effect.

"There's a lost gold mine not thirty miles down the road," said the bartender.

I figured he was about to try and sell us gold pans and metal detectors.

"Down Highway 95, turn right toward Carson's Well. It's somewheres in the Old Woman and Turtle Mountains. Gold laying on the ground, just waiting to be picked up."

"So, how come nobody's picked it up?" asked Tom.

"It ain't from not trying," said the barkeep. "They're searching all the time for the Lost Arch Mine. Four-wheel drives, burros, special metal detectors. They've even used helicopters to look for it. But, nary a speck."

I wanted to hear the history of the gold mine, but first I had to take a piss. Through the men's room door, identified by a silhouette of a cowboy, I could smell strong and abundant urine. The floor was sticky. Could booze alone account for such poor marksmanship? Maybe when a cowboy's trying to pull his dick out quickly from a pair of tight jeans, between chaps, and whatever else they wear, the bladder gives up and sprays the room like a cat.

The bathroom was ecologically correct: no electric, air-blown hand dryers, or paper towels made from trees. On the wall was a continuous towel machine whose towel had reached the end of the line. A filthy rag, mostly piled on the floor, hung from a metal box. It looked like it'd been used to swab out the mare's dock. I flicked my hands on the wall as I compared various brands of condoms in a rubber machine. One prophylactic contained the new miracle ingredient, Linger. I wondered at the reaction of Linger and the saltpeter the Army had been feeding me.

Rejoining the guys at the bar, I noticed most of the stool tops had been slashed. They were held together with tape. Was this the scene of an enormous sword fight between rival tongs? Why would somebody sit on a barstool and slash the top, unless he was trying to cut off his own cock? It was a puzzlement.

If some idiot had done this to the bar stools on Aristotle Onassis's yacht, he would've found himself dog-paddling in the Mediterranean Sea. I read that Ari, an impractical joker, spent a fortune having the stools in his ship upholstered with elephant penises.

They'd anchor the yacht at Monte Lucre or El Goldo. Rich swills sitting in the bar would say: "Well done, old gob," and "Jolly good, rather." If there was a Kennedy on board, the conversation would eventually turn to mountain climbing and saving wildlife: bighorn sheep, snail-darters, and pup fish. The other guests would toss in endangered species: cheetahs, condors, the desert tortoise. With luck someone would mention elephants. If not, Ari would raise the subject himself.

"Didja know," said Ari in Greek-accented fractured-English picked up in whorehouses and ouzo mills throughout Europe, "them bar stools youse is sittin' on was made from elephant dicks?"

In unison, everyone would rise up off their stool looking for . . . a hole? Semen stains? Ari got a big kick out of the reaction. I guess you had to be there. Anyone who knew Ari (he was known as a miserable little bastard) wouldn't put it past him to install air hoses in the bar stools, one end of the hose connected to the bottom of the stool and the other end in a bucket of elephant cum.

Between pouring drafts the barkeep answered questions about the location of the lost gold mine.

"Probably the last man who knew where it was," said the barkeep, "was Death Valley Scotty. He knew every inch of the desert. When old Scotty was pressed for some cash, he'd go to the mine and take a few nuggets."

"That guy must've been a real dickhead," said L.A. "I'd take it all."

"Me, too," I added.

"I think you boys would've liked Scotty. When he was flush, he'd come to Needles and hire all the buggies from the livery stables. Fit them up with red lanterns, ribbons, and such. Then he'd go to the red light district and round up any gals that wanted to go for a ride."

"You got whorehouses?" asked Tom.

"Oh, that was years ago," said the bartender. "They went to Las Vegas and became respectable chorus girls. Pay's better. But, old Scotty and the gals would parade down Third Street, whooping it up. Had a hell of a time."

9

Sitting in a bar, whooping it up in the middle of the day, especially a work day, was a real treat. It's easy to see how somebody could get addicted to this life. The music was great. Roy Orbison—what Okie music should sound like. And that reminded me: no more lunatic wrecker driver. Life was good, and the beer cold. The bartender had enough stories to restart "Death Valley Days" for a few more seasons. This was the real stuff. My beer glass sat on a bar dragged across the Mojave Desert by a team of mules. It was a story that made a person thirsty just thinking about it.

I seemed to be the only one still paying attention to the bartender and his story. My compadres weren't listening, but they were enjoying themselves. Laughter drowned out the music. The tavern had almost everything we could want on a Wednesday afternoon, except "a face on the bar room floor," but it was still early.

What I liked best about our squad was the diversity. We were like those platoons in old Army movies.

We had a tough guy from L.A. who'd say, "So, I axed him, 'How come you don't axt me before you done that?'" L.A. was cool. He claimed the draft board would've left him alone if they had a record of all his armed robbery convictions.

A large, yellow-haired Swede from North Dakota was the biggest cheapskate in the company, maybe the whole U.S. Army. On payday he'd get a money order and send all his pay home. For the rest of the month he'd borrow cigarettes, writing paper, stamps, beer, cookies, chips, whatever anybody had.

Swede would ask, "You got another one of those?"

If Mother Teresa had been in our squad, eventually she'd be driven to say, "No! Get your own, asshole!" In a nice way, of course, because Swede looked like he could pick up a tractor and throw it a fer piece.

There was a black guy from New Jersey who'd steal pennies off his dead mother's eyes as she lay in her coffin. Goldfarb was a quiet guy who had gone to Cornell. Whenever there was a dirty job to do, Goldfarb would disappear. He'd choose that moment to see the company clerk and update his number of dependents. I tried to make Goldfarb's life as miserable as mine. When we assembled for some detestable duty, I'd ask, "Hey, where's Goldfarb?"

L.A. would say, "You axed a good question. Where's that guy?"

After much grumbling, somebody'd say, "How come he don't have to do this?"

Sarge would send someone to find Goldfarb and bring him back.

Williams, a black guy from Alabama, was with me on the Colorado River mis-adventure. We discovered we were both San Francisco Giants fans and became friends. The Giants were my team because I lived in the Bay Area. Williams was a fan because Willie Mays was born not far from his hometown in Alabama.

Williams brought his baseball glove to the desert. In the evening after supper, before the beer trailer opened, we'd stand in the desert behind our tent and play catch. He did an excellent impersonation of Juan Marichal's high leg kick. Then un-Juan-like, he'd bounce the pitch in the dirt. We reminded each other of great players the Giants let go.

"How about Mike McCormick and Steve Stone?"

"And Gaylord Perry."

"Orlando Cepeda."

"Bill White, Jackie Brandt."

"Gary Matthews and Gary Maddox."

"Leon Wagner, Willie Kirkland, Bobby Bonds—a whole outfield."

"How about this outfield: Felipe Alou, Matty Alou, Jesus Alou? And for a pinch hitter, throw in Manny Mota."

Even without the Giants connection, Williams was my friend. He helped me change a flat tire on my truck. He helped everybody. The only guy who didn't like him was Miller, a closet racist. He was a sandy-haired, normal looking white guy. There were no swastikas or chains hanging in his wall locker, no piles of Nazi pamphlets.

At Christmas I went home on leave. Williams asked to borrow my phonograph. I said sure. When I got back, Miller approached me.

"How come you let that nigger use your phonograph?" asked Miller. No one else was around.

I wish I could say I flattened Miller with a hard right to his honky gobstopper. But I didn't. I was too surprised at his question.

"What do you care who I loan my phonograph to?" I said.

"Heck," said Miller, who rarely swore, being against his religion, "for a whole week all he played was nigger music."

I knew the albums Williams had; he'd loaned me some.

"You don't like Sarah Vaughn, Ray Charles, Aretha Franklin?" I asked.

"I can't stand that shit."

10

Curtis Smith, from Texas, had a large tattoo on his forearm. His initials were encircled by an ivy wreath. One day after lunch the squad was lying around waiting to go back to the motor pool. L.A. said, "Hey, you know what CS stands for?"

"Yeah, I know what it stands for. It's my name," said Tex.

L.A. said, "I did not axe if you knew what your name was, did I? I axe if you knew what CS stands for?"

"So, tell me," said Tex. "What's it stand for?"

"It stands for . . ." said L.A., suddenly more tactful than I'd ever seen him. "And, you can axe anybody here if I'm lying. It stands for chicken shit."

L.A. saw the look on Tex's face. "Axe anybody. Am I right?"

Tex looked at me.

"Hey, that's what it stands for," I said. "It's got nothing to do with you."

Tex nodded. He could take a joke as well as dish it out. Cooks were his favorite objects of humor. In the chow line Tex would ask a cook if he remembered to spit in the soup and jack off in the cake mix. I dreaded hearing him say that. I felt he was giving the cooks ideas. After a while no one seemed to pay any attention. Except for a cook from Indianapolis, we called Crash. In the best of times Crash was not a nice guy. Then, while in the desert, he got a Dear John letter from his wife who was back in Missouri in a trailer court. That made him miserable to be around.

Going through the chow line, Tex used to pick up food with his fingers, instead of using a proper serving utensil. The first time Tex picked up a slice of bologna in front of Crash, he was warned, "Don't touch the food with your filthy hands, you okie asshole." Crash's reaction came hard on the heels of his having been asked if he'd jacked off into the cake mix today. Tex tried to correct the error in geographical reference. But, any place south of Louisville was okie country to Crash.

Once Crash warned me as I reached for a piece of celery. "Listen, four-eyes, I don't care if you pick up the food with your sphincter—when I'm not here. But, don't touch nothin' when I'm on duty."

It seemed that one day Crash let a soldier pick something up by hand without correcting him. The incident was witnessed by somebody from the inspector general's office. A report was filed. Crash was called before the company commander. A letter of reprimand was placed in his 201 File. Crash was a lifer; when he re-enlisted, he'd ask to have the letter removed. Having a reprimand thrown out was an understandable request.

Something dangerous was going on behind Crash's wrinkled, little forehead. Everyone but Tex could see the wheels falling off and the cogs jamming. One desert day at lunch/dinner we were filing through the chow line. Crash was standing behind the hard-boiled eggs. He looked as though he'd been re-reading the letter from his wife. Tex had a silly smirk, as if he was about to do something stupid. In front of Crash, Tex reached out with his fingers to pick up an egg. Crash, holding a carving knife behind his back, stabbed Tex's hand. The table had a metal top, so the knife sort of rebounded. Crash could have thrown the knife away and no one would have been the wiser, except for blood spurting on the eggs, and the hole in Tex's hand, and Tex's big mouth.

The company commander gave Crash an Article 15, a punishment less severe than a court martial. He must have considered Crash's personal trauma. The fact that Tex was the victim didn't hurt his case either. Crash would just have the Article 15 removed from his file, along with the letter of reprimand, when he re-enlisted.

11

I don't know whose idea it was to leave the bar in Needles. Our squad leader, Audie, probably made the command decision. That's why he was a buck sergeant and we were privates. We staggered out into the bright afternoon sun. I'd completely forgotten about the laundry. Our teetotaling friends had taken the clothes from the washers, put them into dryers, then into bags. They loaded the bags in the truck and sat in the back. The driver had accidentally parked the truck in the shade.

While nobody was falling down drunk, no one was feeling any pain either. Except for L.A. Something I'd said in the bar had upset him. When we returned to camp, as I jumped from the back of the truck, L.A. jumped onto my back, knocking me to the ground. He punched me and began biting the back of my head. I had no idea who it was, only that it was a serious lunatic. That someone would bite a head that hadn't been washed in . . . three, four weeks, meant I was grappling with a nutcase. The squad, led by Audie, stood and watched.

Later, I tried to reconstruct what I might have said to offend L.A. I didn't say anything. I wasn't even sitting near him; we were several stools apart. After the barkeep ran out of stories, I began my James Cagney, cheap hoodlum impersonation. I bought a cigar from a box of Roi-Tans near the cash register. My pronunciation improved with a cigar stuffed in the corner of my mouth.

"Nobody axe me, nyaah, but if one of youse mugs axe me, nyaah, I'd axe the bartender: 'What kind of rotgut is this, that we're pouring down our beerholes?'" I'm having a little fun. Big deal.

So, I'm lying face down in the desert; L.A.'s on my back biting my head. He could bite better than he punched. A mouthful of dandruff was too good for a back jumper. I flipped over, rolling him off. He was trying to knee me. I tried to punch him in the face a couple of times. He covered up with his arms. We weren't getting anywhere, so I got up.

"Get up, motherfucker," I said. "We'll start over."

L.A. was in the fetal position, arms over his head. "No," he said, "You'll kick me if I try to get up."

"Get up, you prick."

"You'll kick me."

"If I wanted to kick you, asshole," I said, "I'd do it right now."

I took a step toward him. He scrunched into a ball like a sow bug. That's how it ended. I got my laundry bag and went to the tent. My head was bleeding, but I didn't feel that bad. Alcohol can have strange effects. Some guys, like myself, have a few snorts and become the nicest people in town. Others become vicious assholes.

Next morning, sober, I had an aching head. A couple of guys asked me, "How come you didn't throw a stomp into that dickhead?" I wished I had kicked him a few times. Unfortunately, he caught me in a good mood. When word got around that I beat up L.A., my stock rose. Even Crash showed some respect. He started calling me by my last name, instead of four-eyes. There were drawbacks. Just like gunfighters in the old West, I didn't sleep quite as soundly. I listened for noises in the night, such as L.A. leaving our tent, tiptoeing across the desert, returning with a can of gasoline.

12

During the second week in the desert our trucks arrived by train. After they were unloaded, we lined them up in a straight row across the desert using string and wooden stakes. We had to guard them at night. But if someone was stupid enough to steal a truck, where would he find someone dumb enough to buy it? If there were buyers, Yandell would have sold every truck. The nearest large concentration of criminally insane was in Los Angeles, 250 miles west. The thief would be driving an olive drab U.S. Army truck, getting five miles to the gallon. Buying gas for the clunker would bankrupt all but a dentist or lawyer.

First, though, the thief would have to be able to start it. Starting these trucks was tricky. Two important knobs on the dashboard were the choke and throttle. They had to be adjusted properly before the engine would fire up. Once the engine was running a couple of minutes, careful throttling was required before the truck was ready to go.

An exhaust pipe ran up the driver's side of the cab, turning outward at the top. During warm-up, if someone played the choke right while revving the engine to full throttle, gobs of black gunk would shoot out

the exhaust stack. Greasy crud splashed onto the passenger window of
the truck next door, unless, the window was rolled down, or someone
was dumb enough to be standing there. Serious wiping was required to
remove the oily mixture.

If a guy felt lucky, and no sergeant was around, he could turn the ignition key back to start while the motor was running. This caused a loud
backfire; a hairball of crankcase sludge was hurled against the next truck.
Sometimes after a backfire the engine wouldn't re-start. This is what
happened to my truck, old number forty-nine. A mechanic had to fix it,
and Yandell hadn't been replaced. Maybe a third of the trucks were in the
same condition. Each morning I went through the motions, but forty-
nine wouldn't even turn over. Still, every night, we had to guard the
trucks.

Guard duty was from sunset to 7 A.M. when the dispatcher arrived at
the motor pool. Twelve hours were divided among three soldiers: two,
two-hour shifts each. The first shift was best, 7 to 9. There was lots of
activity in the company area and at the beer wagon to watch. At 9 P.M.
you could sleep for four hours, going back at 1 in the morning. Nine to
11 P.M. wasn't too bad, but you had to go back at 3 A.M. The worst shift
was 11 P.M.–1 A.M., going back out at 5 A.M.

The toughest thing about guard duty was finding a place to hide, then
staying awake. We were supposed to walk guard. But walking around
ninety trucks in the desert in the dark is tiresome. It's easier just to sit
someplace. The logical place to do that is in a truck. After all, there was
a whole bunch of them. What were the odds that the captain of the
guard, actually a lieutenant, would drive up in his Jeep and park in front
of the very truck you were sitting in? Pretty good, it seemed. The first
week he caught two guys and gave them Article 15's. If sitting in the cab
wasn't safe, sitting in the back of the truck was out of the question. You
couldn't see the lieutenant coming and climbing out the back with a rifle
could wake the whole camp.

I usually sat on a running board of a truck somewhere in the middle
of the pack. I'd lean back against the gas tank, resting one foot on the
fender, while I propped myself up with the other foot on the ground. I

watched my ground foot to see if something was sneaking up on it—a snake or some other wild varmint. There were no bullets in my rifle, but I could club some critter to death. I watched, mostly listened, for a Jeep, to see if the lieutenant was sneaking up on me. On foot, the lieutenant could've caught just about every guard, on every shift, but he didn't like to walk.

13

One day at lunch I heard about the perfect hiding place. A fool-proof system invented by a guy in the third platoon. The guard would climb on top of a truck with his rifle, and lie on the canvas supported by the wood spars. It's like lying in a hammock, suspended between spars; you couldn't be seen from the ground. If the lieutenant showed up, just wait until he leaves, then climb down and act like nothing happened.

The lieutenant would keep looking until he found you. "Where were you, soldier?"

"I was over yonder, Sir, behind that there truck. I thought I heard something funny going on. Must've been a varmint, I reckon." Unless caught red-handed, we'd come across innocent.

I never tried lying on top of the canvas. I hadn't even got the bugs out of my running board maneuver. It occurred to me many things could go wrong when you're lying on top of a truck being searched out by a lieutenant.

One night the charge of quarters got a call from the train station in Needles; some large packages had arrived for pick-up. Normally a Jeep would be dispatched but, because of the shipment's size, a truck was sent. What were the chances, out of ninety trucks, the one chosen would be the one with a guard on top? The guard could have easily picked a broken truck to sack out on since half of them didn't run.

When everybody got to the train station, the guard on top along with his rifle climbed down. Making a round trip on top didn't appeal to him. A sergeant was riding shotgun, which explains why the guard didn't get down when the truck first started. He tried to justify this action to the sergeant. If the vehicle had been stolen, the guard would've been there to catch the thief. He got an Article 15 anyhow. Some reward for the fact we guardsmen had a perfect record—no trucks stolen.

I continued to slouch on running boards near the middle of the pack. I listened for Jeep noises, and watched for snakes lurking near my foot. It kept me awake. A lesson might have been learned from this, but I don't know what it was. Two quotations come to mind, both inappropriate, from my favorite draft-dodger, Walt Whitman: "Doubt much, obey little," and "No good deed will go unpunished."

14

A new wrecker-driver-mechanic arrived and was assigned to a tent in the fourth platoon. Yandell's old spot in our tent was taken by a guy who looked like an accountant. Instead of regular Army glasses, he wore fancy tortoise shell frames. Glasses weren't completely uncool; Michael Caine wore them. But Caine had a wiry toughness, street smarts, and an uncanny ability to resist torture.

Our new guy was soft in a clerical sort of way. He was older than all of us. He had re-enlisted after five years of civilian life. In a divorce action his ex-wife got the house, car, boat, kids, and a large portion of his salary as a rising young executive for a dog food company. He chose to go back in the Army for fiscal protection. "Fifty percent of nothing is still nothing" is how he put it.

Any day now, Brian, the accountant's name, would be leaving for Officers Candidate School. This miserable tent in the desert was merely a speed bump on his road to the Joint Chiefs of Staff. "The U.S. Army, like the dog food industry, is a numbers game," Brian opined. "Remember that and there's no stopping you."

In previous service, Brian had been stationed at Fort Huachuca in

Arizona on the Mexican border. He went to Nogales, Mexico as easily as we went to stand in line at the beer trailer. Easier, because there weren't any lines. Just a matter of walking across the border. A bottle of tequila cost about the same as a bottle of beer in the U.S.

And then there were the Nogales' women. None of those corn-fed, overstuffed wahines we saw grinding away on "I Search For Adventure." No gap-toothed, tattooed bimbos bussed over by the USO from a court-mandated work release program. These ladies were the most beautiful senoritas in all Latin America. From the very tip of the continent at Tierra del Fuego only the loveliest muchachas migrated north to the frontier.

Brian estimated, in five-year-old dollars, that one could get laid for about the price of one U.S. movie ticket plus a small unbuttered popcorn. That was full retail. For a few pesos more you could get add-ons. One of the bells and whistles involved a second girl; it was called the "Rocket-ship." A nylon scarf the size of a bath towel was tucked into the customer's rectum. The customer mounts the first girl while the second waits behind the copulating couple. Near climax the customer waves his arm and the second girl pulls the scarf from his ass, all in one continuous motion.

The Rocketship was not an experience for the weak of heart. The girls checked customers beforehand, looking for noticeable signs of coronary disease: varicose veins, purple feet, and shortness of breath. For a few more pesos you could do "Around The World," which involved three girls. Any incredible thing you could think of these senoritas would perform, singly or in groups, including multi-species orgies involving dogs and Shetland ponies.

Brian's stories were amazing. We'd lie on our bunks after the beer trailer closed, listening to descriptions of brown-eyed Latin beauties. Sometimes a senorita would fall for a guy and let him spend the whole night. Some guys got laid for free. They'd tell the ladies they were in love and wanted to marry them. They'd bring her entire family to the States, they'd say.

A story one night was about a lithe, Mexican beauty whose breasts were so big she used part of a volleyball net as a make-shift bra.

Somebody asked, "Dag nabbit! How far's Mexico at from here, anyhow?"

Research next day on the company clerk's map revealed we were approximately 250 miles from Mexicali, Mexico. That might seem a long way to a pilgrim, but to an adventurer with his thumb out, it was a straight shot across a flat desert. Five of us decided to go, including Brian, who volunteered to lead the expedition. With his knowledge of Mexico and ability to "habla" he'd see that none of us got screwed unnecessarily. Brian insisted we go the following weekend because after that he was sure to be out of the desert and on his way to OCS.

15

Saturday morning after breakfast, Brian and I, in civilian clothes, stood by Highway 66 with our thumbs out. We were wearing our dog tags. An accident the previous Friday night had made tags mandatory at all times; to be worn outside the shirt so compliance was obvious.

The accident involved five GIs and a civilian who was the brother of one of the soldiers. The brother had driven up from Los Angeles and they were all headed back to the city for some rest and relaxation. Liquids were consumed; speed limits exceeded; loud music probably enjoyed. When the happy group got to the town of Las Pulgas, Las Trampas, or Las something or other, darkest night had descended on the small village without a street light.

In the middle of the road, in the center of town, the citizens had erected a granite monument in honor of the sons and daughters of Las whatever who had perished in WWI and WWII. The two-lane road divided at the rock pile: eastbound lane curving around one side and westbound the other. The car was going approximately 100 mph when it hit the monument. No one was wearing dog tags and all faces were smashed beyond recognition. Identification would have to wait for examination of dental records. The U.S. Army was inconvenienced. From now on tags would be worn at all times, outside uniforms or civilian shirts.

Although we spent two months getting ready, the practice war itself lasted only two weeks. The final body count was forty-seven of us actually killed. The six who died at that Las town were the most in any one incident. More guys drowned in the Colorado River, but not all at once. Some were killed in plane crashes. A couple of parachutes failed to open. Two soldiers were run over by tanks as they lay in their sleeping bags. One guy was bitten by a coral snake. A soldier was shot in the face with a blank cartridge. The shooter didn't have the safety plate mounted on the end of his rifle.

Forty-seven deaths didn't seem extraordinary. There were a 100,000 soldiers running around the Mojave Desert with wild abandon in tanks, planes, trucks, and Jeeps. According to the author of *The Mojave*, the only thing we killed more of than each other was "gopherus agassizii" tortoises. The author accuses us of crimes against nature, suggesting we tried to ruin the landscape. ". . . (A) training exercise that laid environmental waste to . . . the East Mojave." I never even saw a turtle, alive or dead. As my friend Williams would say, "I got your environmental waste hanging, buddy."

16

We stood along the shoulder of the road, off the hot asphalt, on the slightly cooler dirt of the Mojave Desert. Our thumbs were out, pointed toward Mexico. There was no shade; any trees had probably long ago been run over and killed by Jeeps and trucks. The road was flat and straight, ringed in the distance by hazy mountains that looked like fake mirages. Pilgrims wouldn't even be fooled by these hills.

When he was seventeen years old Ed Abbey might have stood somewhere near where I'm standing. "At Needles, California, bound home for Pennsylvania, I stood all day by the side of the highway, thumb out. Nobody stopped." Of course, Ed would've been on the other side of the road since he was going east.

"Needles in August must be one of the two or three hottest inhabited places on earth. A fearful, scalding heat that makes you hurry from shade to shade." You got it, Ed. Things haven't changed.

Mojave looks a lot like Mars with weeds. The weeds are a kind of hybrid tumble and Scottish thistle. Under layers of gray soot the plants' cells may remember they were once green sprouts. They haven't had a drink of water in years. Being in the Mojave is like being in hell without the offset of having done anything enjoyable.

By the time settlers got to the desert they had seen some sights, real and imaginary. Imagine leaving Maine in your covered wagon and clomping on down through New Hampshire, Vermont, New York, Pennsylvania, Ohio, Indiana, Illinois, Missouri, Oklahoma, Texas, New Mexico, Arizona, and finally, God willing, Needles, California. Arriving at Mojave, a certain pattern should've become obvious: places were getting worse and worse. Why go on? Who could have imagined that only a few hundred miles from here lay the future site of L.A.?

But, on plodded the Pilgrims. Some nutball in a covered wagon was the first gringo to arrive at Tierra del Fuego. As the pioneers stood at the tip of the continent, knee-deep in penguin shit, gaping at the huge waves rolling in from Antarctica, a puny voice could be heard: "Let's push on to the next land mass. We can tear the wagon apart and make a raft. Sure to Betsy, there's good farm land just over them thirty foot rollers."

What God-forsaken wasteland would a pioneer have to reach before he said, "Good Lord! Leave us quit this hell-hole and go back to where we came from. At least return to one of the hundreds of fertile, lush, picturesque, habitable sites we passed." A sensibly priced statue should be erected to the memory of that explorer, if such a person existed.

The scenery in the southwest consisted of places later re-named Hot Springs, Cadaver Gulch, Gila Bend, Burning Sands, Tombstone, Dead Man's Creek, Scalding Rock, and Skeleton Canyon. Film buffs recognize Needles as the area where Captain America and Dennis Hophead set out for adventure on their motorcylces in the movie *Easy Rider*.

Brian and I were the only pilgrims trying to thumb a ride on Highway 66. Five guys wouldn't have worked. Who's going to pick up that many hitchhikers? Somebody in an airport limousine, maybe. Tom didn't have any money. Dick said it was too far. Harry decided it didn't seem like a good idea.

"Hell," said Harry, "go all that way for some nookie? You stand at the beer wagon long enough some woman might could drive by and stop."

We pointed out to Harry that we had spent every evening standing at the beer trailer. Nobody stopped; nobody was even on the road to stop.

"You never know," said Harry. "Strange things happen." He re-membered a time back in Minnesota when he was selling magazines door-to-door. One afternoon waiting for the pick-up van, Harry was sitting on the curb in the shade of a mailbox. A woman drove up in a '59 Cadillac with the top down. Her poofy hair was held in place with a babushka.

"Hey, buster," she said to Harry. "Do you think you could drive this thing to Moose Falls?" Harry threw his magazines in the back seat and away they went. On the third morning at her trailer the woman woke Harry early and told him to scram. Her husband was coming in on the 8:35 Greyhound. Harry left so fast he forgot his sampler case and magazines in the car. The magazines were worthless: *Golf Digest, Sewing Basket, Lutheran Voice*. But, the sampler case had a value of twenty-five dollars. Harry signed for it. When he got home he discovered the magazine company had fired him; they wanted their sampler case returned. It was a great disappointment to his parents who were hoping Harry would take his first paycheck and move out.

So, from five horny guys we were reduced to two adventurers. Dick and Harry would be missed; asking Tom to come along was a mistake. This is the same guy who wired his entire paycheck every month to his folks in Wisconsin. He said his sister was in an iron lung, but nobody believed him. His only recreation was going to the PX with a stolen Pyrex coffee cup to get free refills. Tom may have been an idiot but he had sense enough not to come with us.

17

An old guy in a pick-up truck stopped; Brian and I climbed in. He said he could take us as far as Blythe. We mentioned the Army camped in the desert and he seemed to know all about it. A man on the radio was discussing pesticides. Once in a while another guy interrupted to ask: "Yeah, but does it have enough P-47 Zorchatron to really get the job done?"

A paper cup on the dashboard looked half full of cold, thick coffee. The driver grabbed the cup, turned it toward himself, and shot in a gob of tobacco juice. He didn't spit so much as spurt. It was a remarkable shot from a foot and a half away. Too high, he hits the windshield; too low and it's on his arm. Both windows were down, still it smelled like someone had been sick in the cab. Kind of a barfy odor. Maybe something had crawled under the seat and died. I was glad to be sitting next to the door where I could hang out the window and admire the scenery.

The first diorama must've been inspired by a desert. Sky and mountains looked fake. In any particular section of terrain there's a large weed, a smaller weed, and several tiny weeds. A seemingly paralyzed lizard, in a half push-up position, looks stuffed. Sprinkled among small, dull rocks are pieces of soda bottles heaved from passing vehicles. Strange circular

46

objects are tops from plastic jugs.

The biggest defect in the landscape, so far as I could see, was the absence of sand dunes. They were magnificent in *Lawrence of Arabia*. But, we didn't have any. This ground wasn't quite dirt or sand. It's like detritus dumped from wheelbarrows. Soil made from demolished chunks of Seals Stadium, Fleishacker swimming pool, the Cypress freeway. Confetti-sized pieces of shredded library books nobody checks out anymore: *Voyage of the Beagle, In the Deserts of the Earth, Seven Pillars of Wisdom.*

Casualties on the road: snakes, rabbits, skunks, birds; never vultures. Why was that? Vultures spend most of their lives standing on the highway eating road kill, but never get run over. Aren't they ever distracted by a delectable piece of intestine, or eyeball, and fail to notice a speeding beer truck? An enduring myth of nature is that rabbits have blinding speed while vultures are slow afoot. That's why rabbits are plastered over every highway in the West.

Another myth: bears eat berries, avoiding humans unless provoked by some outrageous act. For example, a human picks up a bear cub, tweaks its nose, or like Mo Howard, pokes the cub in the eyes. The mother bear rears up; issues warning growls indicating enough is enough. That's pretty much what our scoutmaster told us before our troop went to Lone Pine in the Sierras for a weekend camp-out. If I'd known bears go into campgrounds, attack and eat campers in their sleeping bags, I'd have turned in my riding crop, pith helmet, Weeblo badges, and play book immediately.

Gorillas, we were told, sat around in expanded families happily munching berries and scratching, leading gentle lives. I suspect anything that eats berries should be watched constantly. A program on "National Geographic" narrated by Diane Fossey showed adult male gorillas grabbing baby gorillas and eating them. Mrs. Fossey couldn't think of a reason why they did this.

Vampire bats, we were told, didn't really harm people. That was an old wives' tale, the result of hysteria generated by Bela Lugosi movies. True, the oddball, aged bat might inadvertently mistake a person for a cow or harbor seal, but after a tentative nibble the near-sighted fellow would dodder off. But one month in Columbia, South America, eight children died from rabid vampire bites.

18

The driver kept his old truck moving at a sensible pace, maybe fifty-five miles an hour. I couldn't tell how fast we were actually going because the speedometer was broken. The odometer and gas gauge didn't work either. He said he had to kind of estimate when he thought the gas was down to a quarter tank and fill up.

We passed a road sign, "Chemehuevi Indian Reservation." An arrow pointed toward the mountains.

When I was a kid, I loved signs and billboards. They were like footnotes in the landscape.

"Just Ahead: Jesse James' Hide-Out. See the cave where Jesse hid from a posse."

"Alligator Prison Farm, Next Stop. This is where Man-eaters go when they're too ornery to go anywhere else."

"See the Snake-Pit. Killer Rattlesnakes. Two Miles."

I think my father grew to hate billboards. He'd stomp on the gas pedal and change lanes when he saw one ahead. But he was never quick enough.

"Lookit, Pa! A snake pit! We've never seen rattlers. Sammy says

they're better than alligators, any day. Alligators just lay there with those dill pickle eyeballs. Sammy says if you get a rattler riled up enough he'll strike the glass."

Once in a while, if the snake farm was next to a gas station, and the gas gauge was on empty, we'd stop.

"Two dollars to look at a snake?" My father wasn't amused. He didn't think too highly of snakes. When he was my age he'd almost been bitten by a cottonmouth while picking berries with his grandma. He was about to reach into a bush for some blackberries when granny said, "Hold on, boy!"

Coiled in the shade of the bush was a big cottonmouth. It was nearly autumn so the snake didn't know whether to shed its skin or go blind. It was doing both. Naturally, the cottonmouth was in a foul mood, ready to strike at anything.

The rattlesnakes were inside a tent next to the gas station. I asked the gas man if the rattlers were in glass cases. He said they were crawling around loose on a dirt floor. There was a wood fence around them. For fifty cents extra, he'd throw in a live mouse.

Alas, no snakes for us today. My father told the gas man he wouldn't pay two dollars to shake hands with Bigfoot. We climbed in the car and roared off, up the road, in search of sensibly priced snake farms.

I'd never heard of the Chemehuevi Indians of the Mohave Desert. I was familiar with the names of many tribes, having spent Saturday afternoons watching Audie Murphy movies. *Duel At Apache Wells* had been filmed around here somewhere. Maybe, it was *Twelve Graves To Apache Wells*.

Chemehuevi sounds like a name given to a tribe in the witness protection program. Possibly, they were related to the bunch who killed Jedediah Smith, and the government renamed them for their own safety. Smith had been massacred somewhere nearby.

I asked the driver what the story was with the Indians and their strange name.

"Nothing like that," he said. "Them's just plain, old Paiutes."

Thanks to information in free brochures I knew that the range of hills off to our left were the Whipple Mountains. Named for Lieutenant Amiel W. Whipple by his friend, Lt. Ives, in 1858. Whipple and Ives were members of the Pacific Railroad Survey. While mapping the area in 1854, they identified some pointy pinnacles as The Needles. The name was later used for a new town on the California side of the Colorado River. Whipple became a general in the Union Army and was killed at the Battle of Chancellorville.

Beyond the Whipple Mountains, Highway 95 crossed the California Aqueduct at Vidal Junction. Vidal was a wide spot in the road, founded in 1907 by Hansen Brownell who named the patch of desert for his son-in-law. The road began to follow the river. We passed the Big Maria Mountains on our right. Finally, we drove into the town of Blythe.

We'd been on the road for hours and weren't even halfway to Mexico. We thanked the old guy for the lift. Our progress had been slow but sure. If Harry had come with us, he'd have used his standard slow-poke remark: "You know, partner, you drive like old people fuck."

Blythe is a hick town named for Thomas Blythe of San Francisco. He bought up most of the Palo Verde Valley, developing the Palo Verde Land & Water Company. The company named the town after Tom in 1908.

Not far from Blythe, on the Arizona side of the Colorado River, is the ghost town of La Paz. Placer gold was discovered in 1862. Millions of dollars of gold were produced in just seven years. Once La Paz had a population of 6,000; now, there's almost no one.

Mining requires lots of wood, so all the palo verdes were cut down. Arsenic was used to separate gold from ore, so the water table was poisoned. The native population was shuffled off to reservations, or shot full of holes. After every resource had been exploited, they closed the mine, abandoned the gravel pit, shut down the company store. Amid piles of rusting equipment, were Indians in mass graves. The brochure didn't say all that; I had to read between the lines.

19

We had a cup of coffee in the Blythe Café. I studied the sun-baked, aged faces of pioneer descendants who ran the town's motels and gas stations. They looked like folks who'd defend what was left of their environment with axe handles. They were discussing a fool communist who'd come in the previous weekend. A tree-hugging Stalinist had denounced dune buggies for damaging the environment. He called it "our fragile ecosystem." Weekend dirt bikers and buggiers were evidently a major source of income. They stocked up on beer and vittles before roaring into the desert to finish off turtles, lizards, and snail darters.

"Hell," said a man in a baseball cap, "Eunice, there, was about to stick a carving knife in that feller's liver." He pointed his thumb at the waitress, a blue-haired old lady.

"You're durn tootin'," said Eunice. "I told that idjit: 'It's supposed to be a free country, sonny. They can ride their motorsickles any goddam place they want. No commonist can tell them any different.'"

The folks in the Blythe Café didn't look like biker fans, but people who drive stationwagons with dogs on their laps. Probably call each other mommy and daddy. I wish I'd known how they felt about the environment. Might have got a free beer with the story of how me and the U.S. Army were destroying the desert tortoise.

You can't tell a book by its cover. My grandfather used to say that. In the book section of the market I'd say, "But, look at the cover of that book, Gramps. There's a picture of a beautiful woman with her bodice ripped open and her ample bosom is falling out. She's laying on the floor clutching the ankle of a man wearing silk pajamas and a smoking jacket. Doesn't that tell you something?" Gramps didn't consider paperbacks to be real books. He felt they belonged in the comic book section. He also advised me to keep my ears open, mouth shut, and nose to the grindstone. He didn't tell me what to do with my eyes.

We finished our coffee and donuts. The lecture on the first amendment had made us hungry; we had two donuts apiece. Standing by the side of the highway, our thumbs were out, pointed toward Mexico. A Mexican family in an old car stopped. In the back seat was a boy of ten or twelve, and a teenage girl. The girl got in front and sat between her parents. We climbed in back and gave the dad a few bucks "por gasolina." None of the family seemed to speak English.

Our desert journey continued. No towns, little traffic, nothing to see but animals mashed into the pavement. My high school Spanish was used up fast.

"Muy calor," I said.

"Si," said father, mother, and son.

Daughter didn't say anything. I think she was mad because she'd lost her seat by the back window. It was very hot, even though all the windows were rolled down. A couple more "muy calors" and we fell silent, lost in our thoughts. The old guy in the pickup had been quiet but he didn't seem lost in thought. He was starved for news from the farm report, and Tractors 'R Us. Maybe this car's radio didn't work. I was lucky I picked up a real estate magazine at the cash register in the café.

A sign, "Palo Verde," flashed by, diverting me from sepia pictures of vast tracts of the Mojave Desert for sale, cheap. Palo Verde was founded in 1903 as Paloverde. Named for a small tree with bright green bark, the original palo is probably holding up a mine shaft in La Paz.

Ahead on the right were the Chocolate Mountains, whose color is a non-chocolate brown. A minor distinction, perhaps, but important when it's all the desert traveler has to amuse himself.

Fortunately for me, the Mexican family was quiet. People jabbering away in foreign languages make me nervous. Once, in a waiting room at the county hospital everybody spoke Spanish except me and Mack. I'd tried to stop my new motorcycle in gravel, fishtailed, and slammed into a brick wall. Unfortunately, the rear wheel of the bike hit the wall sideways, breaking Mack's ankle.

A large Mexican family filled the waiting room: little kids, teenagers, young adults, aunts, uncles, grandparents. It looked like a four generation re-union, where a 106-year-old matriarch holds her great, great grandson. Young people paraded around the room talking in Spanish, laughing, stopping to admire art work on the walls. The art consisted of large framed pieces of bedspreads upon which were awkward farm animals, ineptly crocheted. I'm sure the hospital was able to cancel the art theft portion of its building insurance. No one in their right mind would steal these pictures. Their only possible use would be as blankets, but you'd have to sew several together.

As the teenagers strolled past where we sat, their conversation seemed to be heavy with "pinche cabrons." Several grinning youths stared at us each time they circled the room. We didn't grin back, suspecting that being a "pinche cabron" was not a good thing.

20

At the crest of every rise in the road our Mexican driver jammed the transmission into neutral, turned off the engine, and let the car coast. When our vehicle still had enough speed to restart, he'd shift into gear and turn on the ignition.

After a quiet period, almost like being in a glider, the engine jerked awake with a roar; we accelerated full speed for the next crest in the road. This was the first time I'd seen Mexican overdrive used seriously. We were either going flat out, hell bent for the next hill, or coasting. I wondered how Harry would've characterized the Mexican gentleman's driving? It certainly wasn't like old people fuck.

We coasted into Brawley, a town laid out and named by the Imperial Land Company. A capitalist from Los Angeles, J. H. Braly, bought up the land. Mr. Braly didn't want the town named after him, suspecting incorrectly that not enough idiot investors could be found to make the scam work. He must have envisioned empty cul-de-sacs, abandoned Flying A gas stations, a deserted Giant Orange, missing Burma Shave signs. Biggest possible embarrassment: a pole several hundred feet high with a humongous "Braly" sign with most of the bulbs burned out. The land company respected his wishes with the compromise spelling "Brawley."

Padre coasted into a gas station. While he gassed up, Brian and I went inside the station and got sodas for everyone. A round of graciases and we were off, joining the main highway for Mexico. Lots of traffic and billboards. Padre still used Mexican overdrive but he stopped coasting a little quicker. Cars were charging up on our rear bumper.

Much of the land around El Centro was owned by W.F. Holt. He named the railroad station, Cabarker, after his good friend, C.A. Barker. When a real estate company got hold of the land, they didn't retain the original name, Cabarker—nor did they honor the landowner with Wfholt. Instead, they chose a marketing ploy. The developers wanted to indicate the town was in the middle of the Imperial Valley, which it isn't, while adding a Spanish flavor. They considered and rejected El Medio, En Medio, Ala Mitad, finally settling on the mellifluous moniker El Centro.

We came to the end of gringoland, Calexico: last of the red, hot mothers. Red and hot refer to air temperature. City engineers must spray something on the metal signs to keep them from melting. Calexico wasn't named for a robber baron; I guess they ran out of them. The town was named for adjoining places, California and Mexico. This bit of cleverness is repeated at the Oregon border where a town is called Calor. At the Arizona state line it's Calzona; Calneva's at the Nevada border. Do other peoples of the world do this? In Europe near the border of France and Spain, is there a Spance? How about Sportugal? Or, Portupain? The Nordic countries might have Finway and Norweden. At the border of Turkey and Bulgaria, is there a Bulkey?

21

We parted company with the Mexican family, wishing each other good luck, "buena suerte." Daughter was happy to get her window seat back. The best thing about Calexico is the name. That, and Elmer's Market where free pocket protectors for pens were being offered. We stopped in to get some cigarettes. A closer reading of the store window banner indicated protectors were free with any purchase over five dollars.

Calexico isn't blue collar, it's no collar. Tank tops with comical messages: "Calexico Yhact Club," and "Slim Whitman World Tour, 1953." Many tank top guys were hefty, some probably topping out at three hundred pounds. These dudes weren't bronzed "Baywatch" studmuffins, they were the color of mayonnaise, with huge arms pumped from lifting heavy garbage cans all day. Pony tails could've been braided from the hair in their armpits.

Shopping carts piled high with cases of Grace Bros. beer clogged the aisles of Elmer's Market. The Southwestern sumos and their chunky brides were comparing prices on boxes of cockroach powder vs. spray cans. I thought of my grandfather's favorite joke: "Go to the store and buy 10 cents worth of flea powder, but don't tell them what we want it for."

My formative years were spent following shopping carts full of Acme beer. This must've been before the invention of six-packs because Gramps got quart bottles, called jumbos. He used to buy Acme Beer, licorice, and one small can each of Prince Albert and Half And Half pipe tobacco. He gave me the empty cans, but anything I would store in them reeked. At recess I was the only kid whose marbles smelled of tobacco. Gramps' diet was ahead of its time, demolishing the old wives' tale about a body needing vegetables, fruit, and carbohydrates.

My reward for not climbing into the shopping cart was a piece of licorice on our way home. That was the only form of candy Gramps could leave laying around the house. Nobody would steal it. I didn't steal his beer or pipe tobacco, either. I hated licorice the time I first smelled it. I continued to accept handouts, just to be sociable. One day I couldn't eat another piece; call it anti-social behavior. Risking a broken ankle from a loose beer bottle, I resumed my dangerous practice of hitching rides in the shopping carts.

22

MEXICO

We walked across the border into Mexico, from a town of concrete, asphalt and pocket protectors to a technicolor set out of *Flying Down To Rio*. Street vendors wore bright blouses, serapes, flowing skirts, sombreros. A Mariachi band played "Ceilito Lindo." Someone had the foresight to plant shade trees. The trees were accessible, without iron guards around them. Buildings were made from softer materials, comfortable to lean against. Maybe it was because the walls seemed to be disintegrating.

At sidewalk stands smiling people sold food, candy, toys, homemade trinkets. Gee-gaws were constructed as we watched. Cafes had outside tables with umbrellas emblazoned with Cinzano logos. A guy rode a bicycle. The front half had been sawed off and replaced with a gaily painted ice cream box on wheels. Negotiations were conducted in pig-Mexican— a little Spanish and a little English. Unlike gringo street fairs, nobody got in my face and said, "Hey, dude! Wanna buy a solid gold locket fer yer sweetheart, or ma? Only $199.00."

I saw my first Mexican license plate. Somewhere in the back of my parents' car is a notebook I used on long trips. I listed license plates from other states, commonwealths, and protectorates. Foreign countries were noted along with the provinces of Canada. I never saw a Mexican plate, but I saw lots of Mexicans.

Brian and I were, as my old basic training sergeant used to say, "happy as two pigs in shit."

We went in a bar for a cold brew. The tavern had neon beer signs similar to American bars, except these were in Spanish. Bars everywhere must be alike: provide something to sit on; a flat surface to put a drink on; and that indispensable narcissistic grooming aid, a mirror on the back wall. You can admire yourself while appreciating how much better looking everyone gets as the afternoon progresses. You never find someone in a bar with peanut skins, or other debris, hanging off their face. They're constantly checking themselves in a mirror.

Extra large glass jugs on the counter contained pickled eggs and animal parts floating in a consommé. Bay leaves hung suspended in the gruel while strings of mistletoe seemed to descend slowly toward a brownish muck coating the bottom of the tank. We ordered another beer and a pickled egg.

Two senoritas joined us. Sitting on bar stools, they hiked their miniskirts up to immodest heights. Neither girl spoke much English. They communicated with hand signals. Falsa, the girl next to me, walked her fingers across the bar and pointed to the other side of the room. I thought she wanted to leave and go to a motel. The bartender explained the senoritas wanted to sit at a table where they'd be more comfortable. I checked myself in the mirror for egg parts or bay leaves dangling from my nose. We found a place in the corner where the girls had left their cigarettes on the table and sweaters draped on the chairs.

After a round of draft beers, the senoritas indicated they wanted something stronger. The waitress brought us all hefty shot glasses of tequila, and water chasers for the girls. We didn't know the girls weren't swallowing the tequila. As they pretended to sip their chasers, they were spitting the liquor into the water glasses. We, on the other hand, were tossing 'em back. What was it Poncho Villa said? "The senoritas pretend to drink in sport but the gringos get drunk in earnest." Something like that was happening.

The girls wanted ten bucks a piece. That's half the money I had left. A line from the song "Guantanamara" occurred to me.

"Yo soy un pobre hombre," I said. It means, "I am a poor man from the land of the pine trees." I left out the part about the land of pine trees because I didn't want to confuse the girls.

Falsa repeated, "Norteamericano. Ten dollars."

I said I wasn't a Norteamericano. I was Guatemalan. "Yo soy un pobre hombre de Guatemala."

Falsa said, "Ten dollars."

The waitress brought another round of drinks. We waved her away.

"No mas," I said.

We'd reached a critical juncture. Brian also had about twenty dollars left. We couldn't pay the senoritas ten bucks and have money for serapes, sombreros, food, and a motel for the night. Brian suggested we press on into the interior, away from tourist traps.

We gave the girls our only, last, and best offer of three dollars.

"Norteamericano dollars," I added.

Insulted, the girls left the bar. We finished everything on the table, except the water. I shook all the cigarette packs; one box had some smokes left. I put it in my pocket. Outside the bar, night had descended. We huddled under a street lamp to consider our options.

We could probably get by without sombreros and serapes. Maybe find some girls who'd let us spend the night. But, we still had to eat a few more times. I pulled out the box of Marlboros. Inside were four homemade cigarettes.

"Hey," I said, showing one to Brian, "could this be mary-jew-wana?"

"Nah. They're not going to give us dope," said Brian.

I lit up, took a couple drags, and passed it to Brian. "You're right," I said, "nothing's happening."

I had never smoked dope before. My knowledge of the demon weed's effect was based on the movie, *Reefer Madness*. In the film a character takes a hit on a joint and starts doing back flips up a circular staircase.

Brian took a couple drags and flipped the home-rolled in the street. "Why would those broads give us some joints?" he asked.

"Yeah," I said. "That's a good question."

Just then, from out of nowhere, a policeman walked up. I thought maybe the reefer had kicked in. But, no, this was a real cop. In Spanglish and sign language he asked to see the pack of Marlboros in my shirt pocket. This, I later learned, was "mordida" time. A mordida is a bribe; it means a small bite. Better a small bite than a small death.

Ten dollars would probably have done it. But I asked myself, "Is my life worth twenty dollars? Give all my money to the cop and get out of town?" If we'd been thinking, we'd have seen the jig was up. We were one step past the place Kurt Vonnegut described: "Shoot me while I'm still happy." Brains dissolving in tequila and beer are slow to react and catch on. The pickled egg, my one piece of food in the last twelve hours, was busy trying to soak up all the alcohol.

The cop took us to the police station. We were booked, I think. I'm not sure because I've never been booked before. The whole thing was in Spanish. Our photos were taken. The cop led us to a metal door with a small viewing window. He opened the door and motioned us inside.

The jail was maybe twenty feet square. Four concrete walls and a concrete floor. The ceiling was probably sheet rock. It was like a locker room without the lockers. There were no beds, bunks, cots, futons, roll-aways, chairs; no furniture, nothing. No windows. Light came from a bulb hanging in the middle of the ceiling. Other prisoners were asleep on the floor.

One corner of the room was a recessed shower area about ten feet wide and five feet deep. Shower heads and faucets were missing. There was a water spigot on one wall and a drain in the middle of the tiled floor. The spigot was where we could get a drink of water. The drain hole was where we pissed. A communal bucket was provided to shit in. An orderly emptied it daily.

Once a day, in the afternoon I think, an orderly brought a bucket of something—stew, maybe—and set it on the floor. I never tried any because unless we'd thought to bring a spoon, cup, or plate, there was no way to get the food out of the bucket; and nothing to eat it on. It didn't smell bad. The bucket they carried the shit out in was identical to the food bucket. Occasionally, both buckets were in the cell at the same time, so apparently they were different ones. Most of the prisoners had the foresight to bring bedrolls. Rolled inside were spoons, cups, paper plates, and comic books.

Brian and I found a vacant spot, laid on the floor, and went to sleep. A guy woke me trying to pull a ring off my finger. I sat up, leaned against the wall. I asked the ring thief what he thought he was doing. He spoke a little English and said he needed food. I said he couldn't eat my ring. He said he could sell it for food. Then he asked to buy my dog tags. I said they weren't for sale.

Everyone sat on the floor and leaned against the wall with their legs stretched out. To break the monotony, we'd get up and walk around the center of the room. Some guys spit as they walked. They'd spit next to your legs. If we sat with our knees pulled up, they'd spit on the floor so we couldn't stretch our legs without touching the gob. So we always sat with our legs stretched out. After a walk, we'd return to our spot; stand for awhile, then sit down. While we were gone, some asshole'd try to spit on our place. Going to the shower area was a major expedition: so was getting a drink from the tap or taking a piss.

The first full day, the food bucket came and it was clear we weren't going to get anything to eat. A black guy, a former U.S. citizen, said the guard would buy us tacos if we had money in our wallets held at the guard station. We'd have to buy for everybody. It was best to wait until they finished the bucket. Partner, the name everyone called the black guy, said to knock on the window in the door. He'd translate for the guard, who required a small mordida.

There were eight of us so we ordered eight tacos. Partner told the guard to take it out of my money. Brian and I never had more than one taco per day. A couple of days, when the jail was crowded, we had nothing but water. The number of prisoners varied from three to twenty plus. We figured twenty tacos would clean us out.

The light in the cell was on twenty-four hours a day. Without windows there was no sense of time passing. The arrival of the bucket indicated another day had begun or ended. After four buckets, Brian and I were senior residents.

One day the jail filled. We were packed shoulder to shoulder along the walls. We asked an amigo what was happening. He said it was Friday night. No tacos today. Everybody was in a good mood, laughing and talking; only the deadest, newly-arrived drunks were sleeping.

A tough looking hombre came in. He nodded to a couple of guys. Later, three guys arrived. One of the guys, smiling, went to the hombre and seemed to have a friendly discussion. Then, they squared off in the center of the room. Both appeared to be good boxers, but hombre was better. He landed a shot to the guy's head, sending him through the crowd, against the wall. Without enthusiasm, the guy re-engaged hombre who hit him in the face . . . left jab, right cross, left hook, straight right. Down he went, knocked out. His head conked on the concrete floor.

The fallen boxer's friends slid him to their area and leaned him against the wall. One friend, a big guy, went to hombre and began a conversation. Neither man seemed angry. These were true amateur sportsmen, good losers, and gracious winners. They squared off. Big guy kicked hombre in the nuts. Hombre bent over groaning, but didn't go down. Big guy paraded around the room like he'd won.

Hombre straightened up and signaled he was ready to go again. They squared off. This time big guy boxed instead of kicked. Bad mistake. He should have recalled the sign hanging over the entrance to Arthur Murray's studio: "Dance with the broad what brung ya." Something like that. Hombre beat the holy, living crap out of big guy. At one point, hombre landed a head shot with a cracking noise. I thought he broke his hand, but he continued to bang away with both fists, so something else must've broken.

Big guy quit, still on his feet. His face was covered with blood. He appeared to be in serious need of a physician at ringside. No doctors stood up. Big guy's friend was awake and seemed all right. Now, they'd have something in common. Fights over, everyone slid down onto the floor and went to sleep.

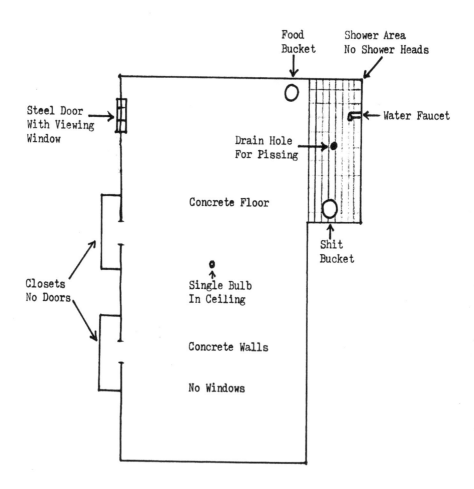

Floor plan: Mexicali City jail.

23

We were the only prisoners from Estados Unidos, except for Partner, who was born in the States but defected. As befits a Mexican jail, everyone else was Mexican. Partner was released two days after we arrived. Without his help getting us take-in food from the guard we'd have been in real trouble. Partner said the guard got the tacos from a street vendor who worked a corner by the jail. I've never tasted anything like the meat in those tacos.

"Gato," said Partner, eating his taco in three bites.

"Good gato," I said, wolfing mine down, too.

We ate gato every chance we got. We drank the water out of the tap, day and night with no problem. Our amigos didn't have Brita water filters in their bedrolls. The Montezuma's revenge thing may be exaggerated.

We told Partner what we were in for and asked how big a deal four joints could be. Serious he told us.

I asked, "What about bail? Even if we're guilty, there's only so long they can hold us. Isn't there?"

"No problem," said Partner. "All you have to do is say the marijuana was for your own personal use. Say that you're an addict. Then they'll release you."

The fifth day, or five buckets in prison time, a guard came in the cell and got us. He put us in the back seat of an old patrol car. I hadn't seen the sun shine in five days. People were walking the streets like everything was normal. A man was reading a newspaper. A billboard showed a lady in her underwear selling lingerie. I hadn't changed my underwear for five days.

The cop was driving us across town when the car quit running. He got out and looked under the hood. He told us to get out and push. We pushed on the trunk of the car while the cop sat behind the wheel, steering. It seemed that the thing to do was run. But, where? Which way? Down the street were shops and stores. Up the street were shops and stores. Where was the border?

The cop had a big pistol in a holster. The possibility existed he was a crack shot. Later, I learned there was nothing to worry about. Guards are issued bullets with half-loads. They have to be close to their target to drill it. I was advised I probably could've outrun the bullet. Still, outrun which way?

While we pushed the patrol car, the guard popped the clutch and the engine started. He set the hand brake, got out, and motioned us in the back seat. Our destination was a government building. The three of us waited in a small room. I thought of what Partner had told me to say when asked if I were guilty or not guilty. "Guilty, your Honor. On account of my being a dope addict." What would the Army say? Fuck the Army.

A little old guy with patches of red hair entered the room and spoke to us in broken English. He said he was related to the Kennedys of Massachusetts. He wondered if we'd heard of President Kennedy. I asked him when we'd get to see the judge. He said he didn't know, and left. We waited another hour. A cop came in and told our guard something. We got back in the patrol car and returned to jail.

I used to wonder at crews of prisoners picking up trash along the side of the road. Why not stay in a comfortable cell? Who needs to pick up empty beer cans, used condoms, and pieces of Kleenex at 6 A.M.? Now, I realize the cell is not a good place to be. I'd pay someone to let me push cars around Mexicali all day. Be sort of a Mexican rickshaw pusher.

Back in jail, we had plenty of topics for conversation. What had happened? Were we supposed to bribe President Kennedy's Mexican relative? Our first and last field trip was the closest we came to seeing a judge, lawyer, being charged, arraigned, pleading not guilty, guilty, having our rights read to us, having the book thrown at us. Why had we gone to that building? Who were we supposed to see? For what purpose?

We should've run for it while we had the chance. So what if we had no money, didn't speak the language, and didn't know where to go. It works in the movies. Besides, the sun sets in the west. To the left is south; to the right, north. All we had to do was hide someplace until sunset, then run to our right. I didn't tell Brian, but I felt we were in big trouble.

Six buckets, no end in sight. When the orderly on bucket patrol came in the cell, we tried to question him, but he didn't speak English. I got a strange urge to know what time it was. Whether it was five in the morning, or five in the afternoon. A new guy came in, slid down and went to sleep. It must have been night.

I used to chuckle at documentaries showing a barefoot native with a bone through his nose, a small Frisbee mounted in his lower lip, standing along the bank of the Amazon or Congo River. The guy was eating a giant cockroach raw, and wearing a G-string that didn't even cover the uncircumcised end of his dick. It's a thousand miles to the nearest telephone, fax machine, or mailbox, yet he's wearing a wristwatch.

The guy glances at his watch like he can't remember if kickoff is one o'clock Eastern or Pacific time. We'd always look for the savage with the Timex, whether it was Marlon Perkins in the Ituri Forest, or Bill Burrud along the Orinoco River. I'd announce to whoever was in the TV room: "See that guy holding the snake. What's he need with a wristwatch?"

I think I understood now. The less you actually need a watch, the more important it becomes to know what time it is. Especially, if you don't know whether it's day or night. It provides a reason to go to sleep.

In the beginning Brian and I talked a lot. We analyzed our situation. We woke up in jail Sunday morning and figured we'd be released on Monday. Our conversation centered on whose parents we should call first for bail. Monday passed. We'd get out Tuesday, we thought. Wednesday went by. The guard took us to an office building; we figured this is it, over at last.

As the days passed, we had less to say. I guess we'd talked ourselves out. For my part, moron's remorse was seeping in. What I'd done was stupid: going to a strange bar in a strange country, getting drunk among harpies and sirens. They were good looking harpies, though. I bet somewhere in the front of Fodor's Travel Guide is a warning in capital letters, surrounded by asterisks. Something to the effect: ***DO NOT GO UNWITTINGLY INTO THAT FOREIGN LAND; ESPECIALLY, DON'T DO WHAT YOU HAVE DONE.*** ***PS. CONSEQUENCES MAY BE HAZARDOUS TO YOUR HEALTH.*** If my worst enemy was sitting here on this concrete floor, instead of me, I'd still be tempted to say that he didn't deserve it.

A prisoner came in looking like a Mexican college student. He wore preppy clothes: a turtle neck with a sweater draped across his shoulders. Everybody else in the cell looked like a bracero, including Brian and I. We hadn't changed clothes, or washed in a week. Rich people didn't seem to get arrested in Mexico.

One of the braceros went over and sat by Jose College. They yakked a bit in Spanish. Bracero put his hand on Jose's leg. He began rubbing his hand up and down Jose's thigh, stopping at his crotch. Jose enjoyed the attention, responding with a little groping of his own. I thought, "My God, they've let a pervert in here!"

The couple got up and went inside a closet-sized room, without door or lights. We all acted as though we weren't paying attention, but conversations stopped; it became quiet. We could hear oohs and aahs. After a pregnant pause, we heard grunting. Next, an odd sound like someone blowing across the top of a large bottle in short blasts. The closet was dark so I couldn't connect noises to any action.

My high school history textbook had a well-thumbed chapter on Minoan fertility rites of 3000, plus or minus, B.C. Rites involving men, women, and horny bulls in some form of dark doo-dahs. The book said that no one knew exactly what took place. How could that be? Somebody besides the bull knew. Wouldn't they tell another person? I sure would.

I'd charge people to see the pictographs.

The textbook didn't tell us what happened because, I assumed, our puny high school brains would snap if exposed to acts of such heinousness. Deeds so foul, not even slasher movies would dare have included them.

I may have misjudged the textbook. Now, I could appreciate the mystery. A Minoan fertility rite could have been going on in the closet and I had no idea exactly what was going on. Hearsay noises do not rise to the level of fact.

Whatever Jose and the bracero were up to ended in a series of farting sounds. Harsh words were exchanged. Jose came out of the closet looking pissed. They sat on opposite sides of the cell. The betrothal appeared to be over.

24

After eight days in the city jail, a guard came and got us. "Finally. Thank God," I said. Now I knew what Dreyfus felt like. I was happy to be released, but resentful of the injustice. Sitting in the back of the police car, I thought up sarcastic remarks I'd make leaving the country. "I doubt that I shall be the last victim." That sort of thing. The guard drove to the federal prison and escorted us through the main gate. So much for freedom. We became federal prisoners.

In the beginning I thought I'd be released the next day. Or the day after that. This was serious trouble and I was scared. But, what could I do? Get off the floor, go to the water tap for a drink, walk back and sit down. My fear was so strong it overcame my hunger instinct. When the guard brought the food bucket once a day, something inside the pail smelled good. He put the bucket down and the prisoners converged on it. I had an urge to shoulder my way in and get a share. But, did I have a share? How would the prisoners react? Without competing for the daily meal their attitude toward me was hostile.

In the space of a short car ride I lost hope of being released. From the city jail, where the only creature comfort was running water, I was taken to the federal penitentiary for hard time. Despair filled me like an anti-freeze.

Just inside the gate, on the left, was a shrine. In the middle of the sanc-tuary was a large painting of the Virgin Mary, in an ornate gold frame. She was standing on a snake. Attending her picture, on either side, were pudgy statues of angels, as robust little children. Even their wings were fat. The angels were set against a background of plastic flowers in water glasses.

In front of Mary's picture were bundles of real flowers. Some blos-soms had been recently placed, but most were long deceased. The dead flowers dissolved into a humus of petals covering the table. The thick humus and lush cobwebs hanging on the angels indicated the shrine has been here for a while. I tried to remember some prayers. "Oh, Lord, in your mercy get me out of here. Never again will I . . ." Will I what? There was nothing I could stop doing that was equal to this situation. What would be a trade off? Something positive. Spend the rest of my life work-ing with lepers in Molokai. Maybe, but the colony was closed. The shrine was nice although someone had too much time on his hands. He should've been digging a tunnel. Still, it was a good sign, better than a skull and crossbones. So close to God, and so far from justice.

The prison was divided into four tanks. Brian was sent to one, I was put in another. My tank boss was Danny Morales. He looked exactly like a slimmer version of Pablo Escobar, the billionaire dope dealer. Black hair, light complexion, neat mustache. He dressed well, shaved twice a day, and spoke English with a slight accent. Altogether, a manly fellow in his thirties. His wealthy family owned a large ranch in Baja. He was serving the maximum sentence for murder, thirty-five years. Mexico doesn't have a death penalty.

Some idiot made an ill-advised remark about what he'd like to do to Danny's mother. A family friend overheard the insult. Danny, accompanied by his ranch foreman, confronted the hombre and killed him. The ranch foreman was also serving thirty-five years in our tank. Most prisoners who get maximum sentences go to an island off the coast of Baja. Reports about the island had reached Danny; his lawyer was fighting transfer.

I was taken to Danny's room, the only single occupancy room in the tank, by his consigliege. Constructed of 4x8 plywood sheets, it held a bed and a small table. There were books stacked in the corner, but I couldn't make out any titles. In a serious manner, Danny explained I could buy a bunk, or sleep on the floor of the tank. If I chose to sleep on the floor, I'd have to work to pay for my food. Sweep the floor, mop up, empty chamber pots, help cook; whatever needed doing. If I bought a bunk, there were no chores and meals were included.

"What's a bunk cost?" I asked.

My parents had often talked about getting a second mortgage to do a few things around the house. This might be a good time to pull out some money.

Danny looked me over carefully. He seemed to be calculating how many pints of blood I might hold. There could be more profit in draining me and throwing my prune-like carcass over the wall.

"Ten dollars," Danny said.

"Ten dollars?"

"Well, how much do you have?" asked Danny.

I said I thought I still had that much money but the police had my wallet. Whatever was in there was his.

Danny said he'd make arrangements to get the money. He told Ramon, his consigliege, to show me to my new bunk.

The walls of the tank were covered by plywood shelves, three tiers high. My bunk, on the second level, was a piece of plywood six feet long, maybe thirty inches wide, with two feet of clearance between me and the bottom of the top bunk.

After sleeping on concrete for eight days, the raw plywood felt like a Magic Fingers waterbed. A piece of cloth, threaded along a cord, could be pulled across the opening for privacy. Bunk owners closed the curtains on visitors day when wives and girlfriends entered the tank. Mothers and sisters visited, too, but they didn't climb into bunks.

Cockroaches traveled along the top of the bunk and concrete wall. When they got onto my plywood mattress, I'd smash them. The guy below said I was making too much noise, so I stopped. It was getting messy anyway. As the varmits crawled into my field of vision along the edge of the bunk, I'd flick them out into the tank where hopefully someone with shoes on would crush them.

25

Next morning, I mentioned to Danny I'd been asking, unsuccessfully, to make a phone call to the American Embassy since I had been arrested. Danny said he'd see what he could do. At roll call a guard took me in the office, handed me a phone, and dialed the American Consul.

A secretary answered.

"I'm an American citizen and this is an emergency," I said. "I need to speak to the American Consul."

After a pause, a man said, "Hello."

"I'm an American citizen," I said. "A soldier in the United States Army. I'm being held in the federal prison."

"Yes, yes, I know all that," the man said. "What do you want me to do?"

"Well, if you know all that, do something to get me out."

"What for?" he asked. "You're guilty, aren't you?"

"No, I'm not guilty. Why do you say that? You haven't even talked to me."

"I'll look into it," he said, and hung up.

So ended my contact with the United States Government; all its branches, departments, bureaus, offices, humane outreach social workers, and support groups.

What would it cost taxpayers, I wondered, to have a government employee sitting at a cheap desk in a small room telephoning newly incarcerated American citizens. The worker, or a calling machine, dials the prison and speaks to the inmate:

"Hey, hang in there, guy (gal). We're doing everything we can. We'll have you out of there in a jiffy."

A generic message of this sort, spoken with the enthusiasm used to sell magazine subscriptions, would hearten the convict. Even if the prisoner suspected nobody was doing anything, had no intentions of doing anything, the call would still give hope.

Potential callers could be recruited from among burnt out welcome wagon ladies and 911 operators. Working with a menu of stock phrases, the caller could alternate "hang in there" with "knuckle down" and "hold that line," maybe "tighten those pucker strings."

But there was no caller/person for G.I. Joe or Joe Sixpack. I suppose if my name were Rockefeller, DuPont, Nordstrom, Sprouse-Reitz, or Eisner, ringing bells and flashing lights would rouse someone at the U.S. State Department.

In the middle of the prison was a large courtyard open to the sky. Flea marketeering convicts set up tables around the walls. After morning roll call, the yard opened; after evening head count it closed. Prisoners mingled all day in the yard, but rarely went into a tank not their own. Regular business was taken care of in the yard. When someone showed up in another guy's tank, there was a serious problem.

The second day I ran into Brian in the yard. He said the guys in his tank hated Americans. He wanted to transfer, but his boss required ten dollars for the paperwork. Later I told Danny about Brian. I said I'd reimburse him ten bucks when I contacted my people. Brian was transferred to our tank that afternoon. A guy loaned him a blanket and he slept on the floor.

Next morning, Brian was called to the office. He didn't come back. I asked Danny what happened. He said Brian was released and had gone back to the States. I was the only norteamericano in the federal prison.

After morning roll call in the yard, we'd go back to the tank for breakfast. The convict-cook for the day heated tortillas and beans. Supper was the same. Saucer-sized, flour tortillas were thick as pancakes. Occasionally, a bit of scrambled egg was evident. Sometimes a piece of meat was diced and added to supper. Whether we had egg or meat depended on what was brought on visitors day. There was no refrigerator so perishables were consumed quickly.

Tortillas were slit across the middle to form a pouch, like a pita sandwich. Beans were stuffed inside forming a small pie. I was the only one without a knife so the cook sliced my tortilla. Some mornings we had a cup of weak coffee; most of the time it was just tap water. Everybody sat on the floor in the clothes they were arrested in, unless a visitor brought someone fresh duds.

While in jail my stomach shrunk. I couldn't eat more than a quarter of my tortilla, usually less. I'd be hungry, then after a few bites I was full. A couple of days with nothing but water seemed to sharpen my appetite. Now, I had good food twice a day and all I could do was take a few bites. Still that seemed to be the least of my problems.

I wrapped the remainder of my breakfast tortilla in part of a paper bag and took it with me to the yard. I nibbled at it until supper. Lunch was not an official meal; it was taken al fresco from assortments found in the yard. My lunch was leftover breakfast.

In the yard, peddlers had set up tables and booths. At night they'd take their stuff back to the tank. Next morning, put it out again. Some stalls had awnings to protect perishables and vendors from the sun. Sellers along the East wall were shaded until after noon. Vendors sold food, clothing, cigarettes, bric-a-brac. We could buy a can of Spam, some wilted radishes, and dope without leaving the yard. No guards were inside between roll calls. Prisoners ran the place.

At the laundry booth, girls washed clothes. They were actually transvestites. From a distance they looked good, until you noticed biceps popping out of their short sleeved blouses. It was rumored they did things beside wash.

Danny suggested I take my clothes to the laundry. For two weeks I hadn't taken off my shirt, pants, socks, or underwear. He loaned me a pair of cut-off sweat pants and an old shirt. He warned me not to pay more than five pesos for the works.

The closer I got to the girls, the worse they looked. Wiry guys with too many bracelets; whiskers growing through their rouge. Except for make-up and feminine attire, there was nothing ladylike about them. If a tough guy contest was held in the prison, I'd bet on the girls. Laundry was done in a fountain by hand on a washing board. Mexican sunshine did the drying.

26

One day I was called to the office. I had visitors. I remembered Brian's last trip. Now maybe it was my turn. Inside the office a man and woman sat on a bench. He looked like a real estate agent.

"I've brought your fiancée," said the man.

"I don't have a fiancée," I said.

"Sure you do," said the man winking. "You remember Doris?" The man seemed to have something wrong with one of his eyes.

Doris smiled at me and winked. She and the man grinned. The guard wasn't even paying attention.

Old time musicals sometimes had a sidewalk scene at a Paris café. A lady in black fish net stockings, skirt slit up to her waist, wore a provocative T-shirt. A cigarette hung from the corner of her mouth.

Doris reminded me of this character.

The Doris in the musical winks at a sailor strolling by. Her boyfriend, played by Gene Kelly, smacks her across the mouth, knocking her off a chair into the gutter. Gene drags her by the hair around the café tables offering Doris to patrons for five francs.

Doris had a cut lip, and bad teeth. Her skinny legs were covered with bruises, injuries sustained, no doubt, from banging into chairs while being dragged around the café.

"I'm sorry," I told Doris' male friend. "I don't have any money." I asked the guard to take me back to the tank.

One day in the yard I bought a cola from a convict at the soda booth. He poured a concoction from an old Pepsi jug into an aged plastic cup. He told me to return the cup when I finished. The drink was tap water added to flat soda somebody hadn't finished on visitors day.

Drinking my cola, smoking a Mexican cigarette, I wandered along to a book stall. Calling it a book stall or soda booth didn't mean they sold only those items. They might also sell lettuce, potted meat, and dope. What this vendor had most of at the moment was Mexican comic books. Among the few paperbacks was *March to the Montieras* by B. Traven. I flipped through the pages; the book was in English. I'd never heard of Traven, but he was about to become my favorite author. On the back cover it said he wrote *Treasure of the Sierra Madre*, which had been made into a great movie. What a discovery!

The vendor watched me closely. Haggling is like playing poker, a shaking hand or nervous tic can betray useful information. I put the book down and acted like I wasn't interested. Magazines caught my fancy: I picked up a *Soapas de Opera*, but the comic book had no substance. I demonstrated to the vendor by swatting the counter several times. I needed a hefty book for killing bugs. Traven's book found its way back into my hand.

"Quantos?" I asked.

"Tres pesos," said the vendor.

At this time a U.S. dollar was worth twelve and one half pesos. For five pesos I could probably buy a signed first edition of *Don Quixote*. We were so far apart, haggling was useless. I put the book down.

"Un peso," said the vendor.

"Bueno," I said. I wanted to ask how one book in English got into a Mexican prison. Maybe there was an American club I hadn't heard of. But I knew he'd ask how one American got into a Mexican jail. I didn't want to go through that again. Each time the story seemed to get longer. And when I asked questions, such as: "How long can you get for four joints?" "What about bail?" "When will I go to court?" They didn't know.

No one knew. It could be serious, they'd say. Without connections, muy malo. In the United States prisoners were filing briefs with the Supreme Court. At the time of his execution Caryl Chessman was considered a first-rate attorney. In Mexico the most precise answer to a legal question was "ah, quien sabe?"

27

Each morning I'd go first to the cigarette booth in the yard and buy two Mexican smokes to last until noon. I'd also buy as many smokes as I needed to repay the ones I'd bummed the night before. I was trying to quit. Why buy a whole pack when the next cigarette might be my last. My system wasn't working; I was smoking more. I'd borrowed twenty pesos from Danny; and the only thing I was spending it on was tobacco. By the time I got to the book stall with my soda I'd already bought two more cigarettes. In the evening before roll call I'd buy eight smokes to last the night. After I smoked those, I'd bum some more.

One morning, changing my strategy, I bought a pack. It was gone by noon. I discovered a valuable side effect of nicotine; if I was hungry, smoking eliminated my appetite. Or, at least I forgot about food for a while.

Part of one wall in the yard was used for a handball court. The criminally insane were housed on the other side. If the ball went over the wall into the lunatics' yard, a peso was tossed over to get it back. One day, Danny challenged me to a game. I'd been handball champion of my high school gym class but I figured beating a tank boss might not be a good idea. I'd carry him to triple overtime, then let him win.

No problem. I got slaughtered. I played as hard as I could, but my speed was gone, along with my strength, quickness, endurance, coordination, depth perception. Even my hand hurt. The ball flew over the wall. I was out of gas. I didn't think I could hit it that far.

Danny threw a peso over the wall. No ball. We waited. The price must have gone up. Somehow the crazies sensed the presence of a rich American through the wall. Unfortunately, the nutballs couldn't observe the happy expression on the poor gringo's face when he realized the ball wasn't coming back. The game over, we quit. Whoever devised the extortion ploy, at the tank boss's expense, probably got the ball shoved up his ass.

I was curious about the lunatics in the next yard. I wondered if the wall was high enough to keep us apart. But how crazy could they be? We had a mass murderer on our side.

28

Sterling, a tall, thin African American, moved to Mexico, becoming a Mexican citizen. He married a local woman; they had four kids. One day he came home, killed all of them, and set fire to the house. He was convicted and sent to the federal prison. Sterling's long sleeve, baggy shirt hung on what had once been an impressive physique. Nobody messed with him.

I wondered if he got one life sentence, or five. He was thirty-something, so even one stretch put him into his seventies when released. He sat by himself in the yard, against the wall in the sun—smoking a cigarette, watching people. After a while, he'd rest his forehead against his arms and knees, appearing to doze. He'd look up quickly, light another cigarette, and gaze around the yard.

I was buying smokes one afternoon when Sterling came to the booth.

"You the gringo, huh?" he asked.

"Yup, that's me." I offered him one of my two new cigarettes.

"Thanks," he said, putting the gift in his shirt pocket. "Come over here. I want to show you something."

Ignoring a direct order from a mass murderer may be worse than beating a tank boss at handball. We walked to his place by the wall and sat down.

"See these people," he pointed toward the yard, at the prisoners shunning him. "They'd like to kill me."

The convicts looked as though they'd like to kill both of us. "Why would they want to do that?" I asked, trying to feign surprise.

Somewhere in the folds of his shirt Sterling found a worn tabloid newspaper. He handed it to me. It looked like a Mexican version of the *National Enquirer*. At the top of the front page was a mug shot of Sterling, next to a picture of a partially burned shack. Down the side of the page were photos of Sterling's smiling family members; their pictures encased in black bands. The word "muerte" was repeated many times.

Sterling pointed at his picture. "That's me."

I studied the text, but the only word I recognized, besides "el" and "la," was "muerte." I didn't know what to say.

"They think I did it," said Sterling. "That's why they want me dead. Her brothers swore they'd kill me."

I almost believed him. I did believe the part about the brothers. "Are the brothers in here, too?"

"No," said Sterling, "but they have friends."

I gave him back the tabloid. The limp paper clung to my fingers like Saran Wrap. Left in the sun for a week, the pages might become firm enough to separate.

Sterling told me what really happened. Basically, it was a misunderstanding.

Some hombres were out to get him. They thought he'd done something against them, but he hadn't. Someone else had. Guys came to his house when he wasn't home. They killed his family as a warning. In order to destroy the evidence, they tried to burn the house down. Sterling had an alibi. He was somewhere else. The police wouldn't listen.

I could believe that. Other parts of the narrative I had questions about, but since it was none of my business, I kept my mouth shut.

Sterling was framed. He identified one of the killers, a man related to the governor of the province. The judge was on the take. Now, wrongly convicted, Sterling sat here waiting for someone to put a knife in his back. The convicts were all yellow, afraid to face Sterling. It bothered him that a prisoner didn't have the guts to stab him in the front.

Fixating on the cowardice of the man who might kill him seemed important to Sterling. Among the problems a convicted mass murderer faced, I'd have thought that was the least of his worries. In some ways, Sterling was just like me, only worse. We were both scared. He had good reason. Any convict could be plotting to do him in.

When Sterling paused in his story, I'd say "jeez" and shake my head. I remember a movie where the warden, a good looking gringo like myself, pretended to be a convict. He circulated among the prison population, listening to just complaints. At the end of the movie he returned to the warden's office and righted all the wrongs done to the prisoners. I wondered if Sterling had seen the movie.

"What're you in for?" he asked. Maybe Sterling was having second thoughts about my position as undercover warden. He could be testing me.

"Marijuana," I said.

"How many kilos?" he asked.

"Four." I held up four fingers. It only works with the number four. If you hold up one finger, it looks like you're pointing somewhere. Two fingers is the victory sign. Three fingers is the Boy Scout salute. Five fingers means stop.

Sterling nodded his approval. At least he was dealing with a person of consequence; if not wardenesque.

Our conversation had taken a direction I was not happy with. I was of the impression that prisoners didn't ask each other what crimes they had committed. Etiquette among convicts in gangster movies, such as *House Of Numbers* with Jack Palance came to mind. Certainly, I could've ask Sterling some disagreeable things. I said I had to buy more smokes and excused myself.

29

Sometimes, in the evening, a group of guys crowded into Danny's small room. I was among the elect. One night we celebrated Miguel's birthday by smoking two joints. Miguel was a guitar player. Besides me, Danny was the only one who spoke English. On these occasions, among his friends, he spoke Spanish exclusively.

I muddled through on what was left of my high school Spanish. Rare was the opportunity to use "la mesa," or "el lapiz." Instead of "wow," I'd throw in "pinche cabron" whenever the situation seemed to call for it. That seemed to be the single most useful expression in Mexico. When someone's angry, it means something like "dirty-rat-bastard-prick." When used as an exclamation of surprise among friends, it equals "holy shit."

Spanish, as spoken by regular prison folk, is tough to follow. Words, sentences come rapidly. I tried to be a good listener, laughing when everyone else did. Marijuana slowed them down, but it slowed my brain, too. An advantage had been lost.

The first joint passed around the room. When it got to me, the third time, molten ash was an inch long. Any remaining paper was obscured by the holder's fingertips. I waved it on to Miguel, the guitar player, sitting next to me. Miguel gripped an edge of paper with fingernails like needle-nosed pliers. He sucked the joint until it all was gone.

Miguel never practiced his music. The only time he played guitar was visitor's day when real mujeres were around to appreciate his artistry. He was terrific. I wished he'd drag out his ukulele in the evening. We could've gone to sleep to the strains of "South of the Border" and "Mexicali Rose." Forget about "Mexicali Rose"; something in the title I don't like. "South of the Border" isn't really a Latin song. It was written by two Englishmen who'd never been south of Twickenham-On-Worchestershire.

One visitors' day I was part of an admiring group consisting of mostly unattached females listening to Miguel play. Finishing a song, he asked what I'd like to hear. I answered "Malaguena," then wished I'd picked something easier. No problem; he played it beautifully.

Miguel suffered from frequent severe stomach pain. He was very thin. You could see the tiny bones in his windpipe. He wouldn't go on sick call. He was afraid they'd put him in the prison ward, and that'd be the end.

Once a week Miguel's mom brought a refill Mason jar of medicine prescribed by the family brujo. If you were within ten feet of Miguel's bunk, you could tell when the cap was off the jar. The medicine was a thick, brown liquid with leaves and twigs. It smelled like rotten garlic, only worse, as though some gland near the anus of a dead hyena had ruptured.

Miguel drank a jar a week. He worked at it daily, taking little sips. It took his appetite away. He ate even less than I did. I wondered if Jenny Craig knew about the formula. Miguel was a terrific guitarist; he could've made out like a bandit with the ladies, except for his breath, and the fact that his mom hung around every visitors' day.

We fired up a new joint and passed it around the room. Some of my Spanish was returning. "Yo tengo calor" means I am hot. "Yo tengo hambre" is I am hungry. Everybody was probably hot and hungry.

The next meal was beans and tortillas for breakfast, unless you'd saved a morsel from supper, or squirreled away a scrap bought in the yard.

Everyone seemed to have something stashed in his bunk. Small wonder the place was crawling with cockroaches. Guys laid on their bunks chewing on old tortillas. But if they had some good food, or a girlfriend on visitor's day, they'd pull the drapes.

I carried my breakfast tortilla around rolled up in my pocket; usually throwing it away. Hot or cold it might've been edible, but hours spent at pocket temperature caused it to taste like a very dead sea scroll.

Danny told a long, funny story. Pinche cabrons were sprinkled throughout. At the end we laughed. I said pinche, but forgot cabron. Then I remembered to say cabron, and quickly put pinche after it. I didn't want Danny to think I was calling him a cabron—a serious insult. Everyone thought what I'd said was hilarious. I laughed too, although I had no idea which part was funny. The marijuana had a serious grip on our minds and we had the giggles. The last joint was finished. Doped to the eyeballs, we went to our bunks. I quickly fell asleep. The cockroaches got the night off.

30

Most evenings, after supper, we sat on the floor and played Diablo, a card game like Old Maid. I hate card games. In order to be sociable, I'd play a few hands. Each player kicked in five centavos at the start. I'd say I had twenty cents, enough for four hands. If I lost quickly, I could go read a book. Every night I'd win. I might lose three games in a row, then I'd win the fourth. Eight players meant forty cents and eight more games. Winning and quitting were considered bad form, so I kept playing. If I was lucky and didn't win again, I could quit honorably after twelve games. Like Vegas, the tank didn't have any clocks, but it was always late. I was tired, worn out from roosting on concrete. I'd climb in my bunk, dispatch a few cockroaches, and conk out. Another day in the bucket.

One morning I woke with a bad cough, and a feeling things were moving in slower motion. After forcing myself to eat a couple of bites of breakfast, I pocketed the rest of the tortilla. Without a belt to tighten, my pants would've fallen down.

In the yard I bought some smokes. I watched as my hand forked over the centavos. Everything was strange; a kind of time warp that occurs whenever I have a fever. Back to the tank for some rest and relaxation. I'd carried *March to the Montieras* around for several days but hadn't started it. At night, after Diablo games, I was too tired to read. Jail, like the Army, has few quiet moments.

I climbed in my bunk and opened the book. The last thing I'd read was a brochure from Needles. I found myself rereading sentences two and three times, trying to make certain I hadn't missed anything. Also, even though I was on page one, I wasn't anxious for Traven's story to end. If you were stranded on a desert island and had only one book to read, which would it be? I could now answer that question: *March to the Montieras*.

Completed paragraphs piled up. I was forced to turn the page. Deliberately slowing down, I lit a cigarette and ruminated. A small bite of tortilla made the cigarette taste better. One thing was clear: this story was going to be depressing. Maybe not in a league with the death scene of Tiny Tim, but close. World class depression.

The story is set in Mexico's remote rural province of Chiapas. An Indian youth leaves his poor village to work on a coffee plantation. The money he earns from contract labor will be used to buy his sweetheart from her father. For his daughter's hand in marriage the father wants "six healthy grown sheep, fifteen yards of white cotton goods, two quintals of worm-free corn, twelve munecas of raw tobacco, and two gallons of aguadiente." It will take two years for the youth to earn enough money to pay for all this.

I was feeling better, more cheerful. I decided to take a few turns around the yard. After one lap the fresh air and exercise sickened me. Back in the tank, I climbed into my bunk and re-opened Traven's story.

After two years, saving eighty silver coins, the youth travels homeward. He stops to eat some bananas in a town near his village, and is cheated out of his money by two gentlemen. The caballeros claim the youth's father bought two oxen from them during the boy's absence. The father said the debt would be paid when his son returned from the Montieras. Pay the debt or we'll call the police threaten the men. It will be the word of an Indian against two gentlemen. The youth hands over his money.

Reading the book, I'd doze off, wake up, smoke a cigarette, take a nibble on the dead sea scroll in my pocket. There was no place in the bunk to lay food where a cockroach couldn't trot over and take a dump on it. My pocket was my food locker. At noon I went to the yard and bought more smokes. Except for being sick, this was the best day I'd spent in prison.

The poor youth of Montieras, working like an undernourished beast of burden, slogging through inhuman conditions, still acted with dignity and honor. Although surrounded by vile hopelessness, he kept the faith. Pennies slowly saved formed a small nest egg. Finally, he had enough money to start for home, again. On the journey he is set upon by thieves who beat him, steal his money, and leave him for dead. Rising from a mud hole, the battered youth must gather his strength to begin once more toiling in the labor camp.

When I said world class depression, I was including books by foreign authors in foreign languages, translated into English. Books forced on me by high school English teachers like *Hunger* by Knut Hamsen; *Germinal* by Victor Hugo; and, a book I accidentally found on my own, *One Day in the Life of Ivan Denisovich*. The title sounded like a comedy. Each of these stories had a central character overwhelmed by adversity, starvation, degradation, betrayal, and humiliation. But it seems to me that all their problems added together are but a stroll in the park compared to the sufferings of the youth in *Montieras*.

Writing contests were held for such things as Worst Opening Sentence, Shortest Short Story, Best Translation, Most Sadistic Teacher, Worst Camping Mishap, Best Imitation of Hemingway, Most Dysfunctional Family. If a contest existed for "Most Depressing Book," *Montieras* would retire the trophy.

The story of the youth from *Montieras* takes a turn for the worse. Conditions become unbearable. The boy's life is hell on earth. It sort of reminded me of my own situation. I seemed to have reached a point in the book paralleling where I was in real life. If our courses were plotted on a graph, they would resemble straight lines plunging downward.

31

At supper I had no appetite. My pockets were full of old tortillas. Soon, I'd have to start releasing them down my pant legs in the yard, like contraband dirt from an escape tunnel. I was invited to a gathering at Danny's room. It was Jose's birthday and we celebrated with a half-pint.

Although every kind of dope was available, this was the first real booze I'd seen—other than a garbage can of homebrew in the kitchen alcove. When I saw the can, I figured it was used for garbage. Then the cook gently raised the lid and gazed solicitously at whatever was inside. He saw me watching and called me over for a taste. Dipping an old wrinkled paper cup in the can, the cook offered me a snort.

I had seen one thing that resembled the mess in the can. A corner of Lake Berryessa, near the dam, is a catchall for debris being pulled toward the hydroelectric generators. In this recessed area of the lake the water is covered with plastic bottles, bicycle tires, used condoms, dead animals, hats, tennis shoes, soiled diapers, tampons, and dissolving bags of garbage thrown over the bank.

The cook pinched one side of the cup to a point so he could skim fluid from the floating and partially submerged rubbish. I took a sip; it wasn't bad. It didn't taste like booze, though. Finishing the cup, the cook smacked his lips and said the brew wasn't ready. I began to notice other cooks sampling the brew; it was never ready. Each cook added something new: eggshells, rotten fruit, vegetables. The gestation period was always being extended.

Six of us piled into Danny's room to drink a half-pint of clear liquid. I figured it was tequila. A couple of sips apiece; hardly worth the effort. When the bottle got to me, I looked at the industrial style label: "Chateau Glycerin." It didn't really say "chateau"; I made that part up. I wasn't expecting Jack Daniels, but this was like drinking gasoline, or paint thinner. At two hundred proof, it was pure alcohol. If we'd been able to send out to the paint factory for another bottle, we'd all probably be dead. After almost two passes around the room, the bottle was a dead soldier. I didn't regret missing my second snort; glycerin burns all the way down and has the kick of a mastodon.

As we filed out of the room, Danny said to me in English, "How you doing?"

"I don't feel so good," I answered, truthfully.

I wondered if we'd have a treat for my birthday, maybe mescal, or absinthe.

In my bunk I didn't feel like reading any more. The poor youth of *Montieras* was worse off than me, but he started worse off. In terms of free falling, we were probably even. He came from a poor village in Chiapas, while I came from a tent in the Mojave.

My situation called for a change of direction. I needed to do something positive, like quit smoking. When I finished my last two cigarettes, I wouldn't buy or bum more. This was good thinking. I lit my next to last smoke. Maybe I'd start exercising, too. I could leave the joint with rock hard abs. Charles Bronson did it in *The Great Escape*. For now, sick as I felt, quitting smoking was a good beginning. Quitting shouldn't be too difficult; cigarettes tasted awful. I crushed this one out on the side of the bunk. Attending the birthday party was a bad idea. I felt worse.

5 Die in Mexican Prison Riot

SWAT team members and police regained control of the Mexicali State Penitentiary yesterday after nearly 30 hours of prisoner rebellion. A fight between prisoners exploded into a riot Tuesday night, leaving five inmates dead and four injured in the second burst of violence at the prison in a month. The prison, which houses inmates convicted of violent crimes, is on a main thoroughfare, just a half-mile south of the U.S.-Mexico border.

When we fell out at morning formation, Danny told the guard I needed to see a medico. I went on sick call. A clerk took my temperature, then a guard took me to the hospital. I was feverish, lightheaded, dizzy, with a bad cough. Mexican compassion for the sick is impressive. In the Army I would've been told by a Spec. 4 that I was OK, except for wasting everyone's time with my malingering. The Spec. 4 would admit he himself was sicker than I was, but he went to work, did his job, didn't waste taxpayers money.

My first experience with Army medicine occurred in basic training at Ford Ord, California. I went on sick call, feverish, with aches and pains. A couple of aspirins, a few hours out of the wind, I figured. They put me in the hospital. When I got out a week later, they closed the base and sent us all home for two weeks. It was Christmas time. What a thoughtful thing to do. Maybe in two years I'd re-enlist.

At home my parents told me they'd read of an outbreak of meningitis at Fort Ord. Four recruits had died. The Army closed the base trying to find the source of the illness.

The guard drove us to the side of the Mexicali hospital, a large multistory building. We walked around to the back. I guessed we were going to use the servants' entrance to not scare anybody. An aide came out of the hospital with a wheelchair and I sat in it. The aide, followed by the cop, pushed me along a sidewalk across a grassy area. The path led through a row of trees and tall bushes that nearly formed a wall.

Ahead of us was an ancient, adobe building. It looked like the barracks at the mission in Sonoma. The sidewalk stopped ten feet short of a heavy, wooden door. While the aide unlocked the deadbolt, the cop told me to get out of the wheelchair. We walked across the rough ground into the prison hospital. Two rows of cots, maybe ten in all, were arranged end to end down the middle of the room. On each bed was a blue and white striped mattress without a cover. Some cots had blue and white striped pillows without covers. I guess the severity of illness determined whether someone got a pillow. On the end of each bunk was a folded sheet. Small, bare tables stood by the beds.

A thin, shirtless guy lay on his back on one cot smoking a cigarette. His side table held a pack of smokes and a book of matches. When we entered the room, he didn't even glance over. A sheet covered his body from the waist down. One bent knee pointed at the ceiling. He almost looked like Miguel, the guitar player. His moustache was droopier than Miguel's, making him look like a bandito. The aide told me to pick a bunk. I chose one farthest from Bandito. The cop and aide left, locking the door.

Lying on my filthy mattress, I gazed out through a row of tall windows along one wall. I could see trees, bushes, and part of the regular hospital's roof between branches. There was no glass in the windows, but iron bars were mounted outside the openings. Graffiti covered the walls: poems, names, dates.

At least I wouldn't have to play any crummy card games, unless Bandito had a deck hidden under the sheet. I don't think Diablo can be played two-handed, anyway. I wouldn't be tempted by cigarettes, except for the pack on Bandito's table. Luckily, I didn't have the urge to smoke. Sickness must short-circuit the desire. I remember reading that Humphrey Bogart quit when he learned he had lung cancer. Or maybe it was Gary Cooper.

Serious illness can be a motivation. John Wayne got lung cancer, quit smoking, and lived several years more. Still, if Bandito had offered me a smoke, I'd probably have taken it, just to be sociable.

I pushed myself up and walked to the windows in order to show Bandito I could still move. I wasn't a person to be trifled with. The iron bars on the outside of the windows were an inch thick. I tugged at them, like a shopper might half-heartedly kick the tires on a used car.

The bars weren't far enough apart to crawl between, or Bandito—thin as a rail—would already be gone. I couldn't tell where the fasteners were located, whether each bar was mounted separately, top and bottom, or the bars were welded to a frame with bolt holes spaced around the grid. If a revolution broke out, we'd be protected. Cannon balls would bounce harmlessly off this iron.

Graffiti on the walls consisted of messages. They commonly began "Recuerdo . . ." and ended with a person's name. Most of the writing was on the wall that had the windows, probably chosen because of the inspiring view. Trees are incredibly beautiful after staring at concrete for weeks. Even bushes should have poems written about them. The writer's impulse must be similar to the urge felt by people jumping off the Golden Gate Bridge. All but one person chose to jump off the east side of the bridge, facing the beautiful city.

The names remembered on the wall must be guys who died in this room. Where else would they have died? How else would the writers have known without radio, TV, newspapers? This was the end of the trail. And what happened to the guys who wrote the messages?

At one end of the room was a toilet and sink. I got a drink of water from the faucet and went back to my cot to lie down. I didn't feel too good. Just to pass the time I tried to think of the stupidest thing I'd ever done besides going to Mexico. I remembered leaving my book, *March to the Montierrias* back in the tank. I was pretty sick to forget my book. Some asshole would steal it. I'd never find out what happens to the youth of Monterrias. The ending, I suspected, was not happy.

It was getting late. They forgot to give us dinner, or supper, whatever they call it. It didn't matter, I wasn't hungry. All I could see of the trees was their silhouettes against the sky. They reminded me of pine trees. We had driven through a forest of them when I was a kid.

The road divided in two, each side disappearing among the trees. At a fork in the road a parking lot had been created by clear cutting the forest. We parked and got out of the car to stretch our legs. Visitors were admiring a large billboard on which a map of the area had been hand painted. In the center of the picture was a lake surrounded by trees. Each tree was meticulously drawn. The artist either loved this place very much, or was paid by the hour.

On the map the divided road went around the lake. Either direction you'd eventually return to this spot. Where we stood was indicated on the picture by a blank spot, dirt colored. A sign sticking in the map's parking lot said "You Are Here." I looked around for the smaller sign but saw only the billboard.

Standing in the parking lot on the map, you could easily see the lake. Tiny waves were lapping at the bare ground. Here, in the real lot, our view of the lake was blocked. A row of trees stood at the back of the parking lot. A magnificent view of the lake ruined by an incompetent builder.

Someone in the crowd suggested maybe the contractor ran out of money. Another man, who looked as though he knew something about incompetence, said even a moron would have sense enough to start cutting next to the lake. That way any trees remaining would block the view of the crummy road. A sensible idea, although the road was no crummier than most we had traveled.

On the map several campgrounds were indicated along the road: groups of tents painted olive drab. Larger camp sites had markets selling bait, sodas, and beer. The biggest village on the left of the lake was Bear Hollow; on the right, Trout Camp. At the far end of the lake was Fern Canyon with a small user friendly waterfall.

I wondered if a rivalry existed between sides of the lake. Did Bear Hollow meet Trout Camp in a football game, or tug of war? Maybe they rowed out to the center of the lake in canoes and bicycle boats, trying to vanquish their opponents with oar shots to the head. The winning team got to throw the losing camp's homecoming queen in the volcano. Today could be the day for the annual mano a mano; it's possible. There was a lot of information printed at the bottom of the map. I checked the dates under special occasions and festivals.

We weren't going to drive by the lake. We'd never see Bear Hollow or Trout Camp. We had come twenty-eight miles out of our way, down this road, because a line on our road map appeared to be a short cut to another road. The line wasn't a road but a creek leading from the lake. On the billboard map we could clearly see this road didn't connect with any other.

If somebody asked me what we ought to do next, I'd say, "Let's stay here." We could go to Bear Lake or Trout Camp. There's hiking trails and boat rentals. The markets sell beer and worms, so they must sell candy and comic books. The place had everything, a perfect vacation spot dumped in our laps.

I'd go to Fern Canyon, stand in the pool below the waterfall, and let the water splash on my head. The only waterfall I've seen was at Yosemite. I couldn't tell whether it was five miles away or fifty; the water didn't seem to move. At night we watched firefalls from the parking lot. They pushed a load of burning logs over the falls.

Some guy said it wasn't being dumped over the falls, it was dumped down the face of the mountain. Nobody believed his story.

A guy wearing a Robin Hood peaked cap said, "So, that way they can set fire to the whole goddam place every night, I guess." He had a large feather in his cap, which he claimed was a tail feather from a condor he shot while duck hunting.

A man in a green baseball cap with a Sierra Club logo said that condors were a protected, endangered species.

The guy in the Robin Hood cap said he was only kidding; the feather came with the hat. He didn't know what kind of bird it came from but he knew one thing for certain: "They don't shove a truck load of goddam burning logs off a mountain top into a valley when there's a perfectly good waterfall they could use."

Instead of showing us training films about heat prostration, the Army ought to have shown movies about how to break out of jail. I'd have to talk to Bandito about forming an Escape Committee. Now that there were two of us, we should have a plan.

A good night's sleep. Next morning I felt better. Fresh air circulating through the open windows was invigorating. It could be part of a new, advanced treatment. The cigarette pack was still on Bandito's table. I thought, since he hadn't killed me during the night, maybe he'd loan me a smoke.

"Por favor, amigo," I said.

He didn't answer. Bandito was still lying with his knee pointed at the ceiling. I didn't pursue the cigarette. Friends don't wake friends early in the morning. I watched the trees light up from the top down.

An aide unlocked the door. It was the same one as yesterday. He went to Bandito's bed. The guard stood outside the room. The aide talked to Bandito, asking him questions. Bandito didn't answer. The aide left. He came back with a guy pushing a gurney. They pulled the sheet over Bandito's head, picked him up like a statue, and laid him on the cart. His knee was still bent, pointing upward. While the other guy maneuvered the cart toward the door, the aide came by my bed.

"I'll be back," he said. Or, "I'll return soon." Something like that, as if it mattered.

I'll wait here until you get back, I thought.

Despite the tragic aspects of the situation, all I could think about was the pack of smokes laying on the side table. On the way out, the aide picked up Bandito's cigarettes and matches. Who would write Bandito's "recuerdo"? Not me, we weren't that close. I didn't even know his name. Let the aide write it, since he got the smokes.

33

The aide came back accompanied by a nurse, a real girl-nurse in a white uniform. She was about eighteen, short, attractive in a full-figured way, and had a cute smile. While taking my temperature, she held my wrist, checking for a pulse. This was my first female contact since . . . I couldn't remember. Then, I remembered.

Home from basic training after getting out of the Army hospital, I met a lady at a trailer court managed by my uncle. LaDonna came into my uncle's mobile home to pay her space rent. She and I chatted; I invited her out for a drink. We went to a few bars, then back to her trailer. We smooched on the sofa while her two teenage kids wandered around. LaDonna was thirty-five or forty. When her kids went out for the evening, we moved to the bedroom. She didn't want to set a bad example for her children. Being twenty-two and impressionable, I admired character in a woman. I saw LaDonna once more, then it was back to basic training at Ford Ord.

The following week I was on sick call with a raging case of crabs. A medical clerk told me a crab joke: How do you get rid of crabs? Answer: Set fire to your pubic hair and when the little suckers run out on your dick, stab them with an ice pick.

"We need to know who you've had sexual contact with," said the medical clerk. "Everything will be kept strictly confidential. It's required information for a sexually transmitted disease survey."

"We're not talking disease here," I said, "only infestation."

The clerk insisted on the name, or names.

I could see truck loads of MPs arriving at my uncle's trailer court, wrapping yellow warning tape around everything. My lady friend brought out in handcuffs; her children mortified. My uncle pissed off because Army trucks were blocking the driveway, and he couldn't get his car out to go buy another six-pack.

"Nobody," I said to the medical clerk, "that's who I had sexual relations with."

A lovely senorita named Alma was holding my hand, actually my wrist, speaking to me in romantic Spanish.

"Donde esta duella?" she asked.

I pointed to my chest. "There," I answered.

She put her hand on my chest. "Alli?"

I adjusted the location a few millimeters, leaving my hand on hers. I wish I'd taken a sponge bath in the sink last night. But, how was I to know this was going to happen. If it was happening? Maybe Alma appeared to Bandito last night just before he died, too.

The aide stuck his head in the door and yelled something like, "Hurry up!"

In a firm voice I think Alma said, "Mind your own business."

After awhile, the aide complained that he needed to leave. Alma said she'd come back to see me. She squeezed my hand, and left. This, I suspect, is as good as it gets in a Mexican prison hospital.

I considered the possibility I was hallucinating. Maybe I was having an out-of-body experience. But if an angel was coming to get me, why would she bring a sleeze-ball, cigarette thief like the aide? Only in real life could I find such characters. Furthermore, we made flesh to flesh contact. In twilight-zone, white-light situations people run toward each other in slow motion, reaching out but never actually touching.

Late that afternoon Alma returned. I didn't see the aide. The guard waited outside. She brought buttered tortillas wrapped in a linen napkin, and a plastic drinking cup.

She checked my pulse. Her hands were very soft.

"Quantos años?" I asked.

"Nineteen," she said, I think. She asked how old I was.

"Veintidos," I answered. I asked if she was studying to be a doctor. Not knowing the word for intern, I used the jail term "brujo."

"No," she said, laughing. She was studying to be a nurse.

This simple exchange might take a minute in one language, but Alma spoke less English than I spoke Spanish. We labored over each word other than "and" and "the." I wasn't certain whether she said nineteen, thirty-nine, or fifty-nine years of age. She spoke very quickly. I know it ended in a nine. Our questions and answers required patient re-translations, but we didn't care.

"Como se dice?" is a valuable Spanish expression. It means "how do you say?" If I reached a point in a sentence where I wasn't sure of the translation of a word or phrase, I'd use "como se dice" followed by the word in English and/or pantomime.

I remembered enough high school Spanish to use "tu," personal and intimate rather than the formal "usted." Polite words of conversation returned: "estudiar," to study; "lindo," lovely; "muy guapa," very beautiful.

In the tank it was chingas this and chingas that. Sentences begin and end with pinche cabron. Not that I minded. It was like being in the Army again. A natural form of conversational Spanish.

Now I had to weed the chingas from my vocabulary, along with cobarde, puta, pinche cabron; some others I wasn't sure of. As long as the word was clean, the exact translation wasn't important. Nineteen, or thirty-nine? What difference does it make if you're in love?

34

Next morning, I was back in federal prison, feeling much better. Fresh air pouring through open windows twenty-four hours a day must be good for what ails you. Alma's lovely presence, and her special buttered tortillas, helped my recovery. I looked forward to getting my hands on a cigarette. I had asked Alma if she had any smokes. She said they were bad, "muy malo."

Some convict had moved into my bunk and was living there. I think his name was Rodrigo. He wasn't one of the regular Diablo players. I went to see Danny.

"What's that guy doing in my bunk?" I asked.

Danny said, "Rodriguez claimed it."

"How could Rodriguez claim my bunk?" I asked. "You said I bought it for life."

"We didn't think you were coming back." Danny loaned me a blanket to lay on the floor, where I'd be sleeping with the campesinos. From the penthouse to the outhouse, how low the mighty had fallen.

I asked Rodriguez, "Where's my book?"

"Somebody must of stole it," he answered.

I knew he'd say that. The only person in the tank who read anything stronger than comic books was Danny. I'd offered to give him the book when I finished it. That means the thief was a non-English speaking, comic book reader. The book didn't have pictures.

My parents wrote to me once a week when I was at the Army post. I'd call home every week, collect; writing monthly, more or less. I'd written from our camp in the Mojave Desert, so my parents had my last address. When several weeks passed without collect calls, they became suspicious. My mom knew something was wrong.

They called Fort Leonard Wood, gave the desert camp address, and asked for our company's phone number. Many calls later they reached battalion headquarters and got the number for my company. Our first sergeant told them I was AWOL in Mexico. He suggested they speak with someone at the adjutant general's office.

A colonel at AG explained what he knew of the situation: I was in jail in Mexico. My parents said the Mexicans must have made a mistake. They arranged to meet the colonel in Needles the following weekend.

At the meeting my parents were told where I was, how to get there, and the name of an American attorney in Calexico. The lawyer's name had been recommended to the colonel as he gathered information about the case. My parents planned to go to Mexicali the following weekend.

They called the lawyer in Calexico; he wanted a substantial retainer. They said they'd give him a check next Saturday in person. The lawyer said he worked hand in glove with a Mexican attorney across the border. The fee covered the cost of two lawyers working on the case. It appeared to be a serious and difficult matter, but he felt certain they could resolve it.

The day after I got out of the prison hospital was visitors' day in the tank. I had my first real visitors: my mom and aunt. Men visitors weren't allowed. My father waited outside in the rented car. Mom said the U.S. Army was doing everything it could. My parents had called our congressman, George Miller, who was doing everything he could. An American and a Mexican lawyer had been hired, and they were hard at work on the case. Our American attorney said the Mexican attorney said the case looked very hopeful.

If I'd known my mom and aunt were coming to visit, I might've worried a little about the reaction in the tank. We were the only gringos. I was relieved. The other convicts were busy with their visitors. Everyone was either polite or indifferent.

I introduced Danny who was his usual gracious self. My mom found it hard to believe he was a prisoner. She thought he was part of the staff, the vice-warden, maybe. After Danny moved on to another group, she remarked how well dressed he was, how gentlemanly he acted.

"Well, he is a gentleman," I said. "And the guy he killed was a dirty rat who probably needed killing."

I told my mom how Danny took a napkin from his pocket after every meal and polished the front of his teeth. This was in addition to brushing twice a day. He showed me how to re-sharpen a dull razor blade by sliding it around the inside of a water glass.

Danny's family never visited. His only occasional visitor was the secretary of his abagado, a Mexican lawyer. Danny strolled around the tank greeting prisoners' wives, girlfriends, and relatives. He was treated with great respect by everyone. Danny was the only one who could get Miguel, our temperamental guitarist, to perform when he didn't feel like it.

Miguel didn't feel well the day my mom visited, but Danny got him to play "Malaguena" anyway. He was terrific. He didn't use a guitar pick. Maybe that was the secret to this beautiful music. Miguel didn't need a pick. He had fingernails like a cheetah's claws, long and pointy. I suggested to Danny that when Miguel was feeling better we should get him to play "Buenaguena." My joke got a small smile from Danny.

As my mom and aunt left, Ma gave me a twenty-dollar bill folded over several times. Most of it was used to repay Danny for sums advanced for cigarettes, sodas, and Brian's tank transfer fee. I thanked them for coming to see me. Ma said they'd be back the following weekend, or the next, depending on what the lawyer had to say. When they left the jail, my father drove them to the courthouse in Tijuana to hand deliver some papers the attorney said were urgent. It was a long trip home so my father could get to work Monday morning.

"Take care," said my mom.

"Bye, Ma," I said. "Bye, Aunt Ann."

I don't think my aunt said one word the whole time. She may have been in shock: prisoners walking around loose, no guards. Her idea of visitors' day at the slammer was formed by watching James Cagney movies:

Prisoner shuffles into the room wearing bowling balls chained to his ankles. Guards wearing thick, blue woolen uniforms nervously finger triggers on machine guns. The convict slumps onto a stool behind a bullet-proof glass. Above the partition, extending to the ceiling, is a heavy wire mesh, the kind used to separate gravel at the Boulder Dam.

The visitor talks through a tube system as intricate as those designed to send invoices between departments at Macy's. The visitor is groggy from a strip search. Guards probed their naked person for concealed weapons, rolled-up obscene magazines, hacksaw blades, and Warding Bastard files.

Mexican penology is very simple. They eliminated guards, ankle chains, gun towers, cell checks, and uniforms. If one is arrested in his birthday suit, that's what he wears. They didn't need rubber hoses, thumb screws, or cattle prods, because everyone was considered guilty. Nobody had ever even asked if I was guilty. Paperwork must be easier for clerks because they have half as many boxes to check.

Mexican jails spare visitors humiliating physical examinations. As a result, paper books in English are one of the few items that couldn't be found in abundance. Guards stayed out because it was too dangerous inside. It wasn't necessary to smuggle anything into the tank when we could go to the yard and buy whatever we needed. Files, bolt cutters, a chainsaw might be special order. However, what convicts want is not Warding Bastards, but dope.

What I first thought to be dope addicts stoned out of their gourds turned out to be just that. Regular convicts avoided them. I was advised they were capable of every treachery. Drug addicts were the worst of the lot. Murderers were the best. They kept their word; they didn't steal much; they acted honorably. If there was a problem, the murderer straightened it out face to face. The dope addict snuck around in the dark with a knife.

I was told that Carlos, a guy in our tank, had taken my book. He tried to sell it in the yard. Nobody wanted the English book unless I'd buy it back. I said I didn't want it. It was a bad book, "mala puta."

Carlos had seemed kind of slow, retarded, I thought. Actually, he was a heroin addict, stoned all the time. He had tattoos around his neck and on the inside of his forearms past the elbows. These were areas where he shot up. A couple of tattoos on his forehead and he'd be a dead ringer for Queequeg in *Moby Dick*.

35

Wednesday was visitors' day. I cleaned up and stood by the entrance with the other guys, watching the ladies arrive. Many were pretty. I'd smile. Some ladies would acknowledge me with a nod.

I'd say, "Como esta?"

A few smiled back, "Bien, y usted?"

Most of the ladies were either wives or girlfriends, so I had to be careful. I tried to act sociably, rather than seem lecherous. Although in my heart I had lustful intentions.

Miguel's mom, carrying a re-fill jug of garlic juice, asked if my mom was going to visit. I said no, but thanked her for asking. The safest course is to thank everybody for everything, even if it made no sense. Given the opportunity, I'd probably thank Carlos for stealing my book.

The last of the visitors straggled in. Among them was a lovely senorita wearing a flowery blouse and black skirt. Without her white cap and uniform I almost didn't recognize Alma. Her hair had been tucked under her cap; now it was long and down her back.

"Como esta?" I asked.

"Muy bien," Alma answered. "Y tu?"

It occurred to me she may have come to see someone else. But, other than the dead guy, I had been her only patient at the prison hospital.

"Why are you here?" I asked.

"To see you," she said.

Danny stopped by. I introduced him to Alma. They exchanged pleasantries.

"If you'd like to visit in the privacy of my room," said Danny, "I'm not using it." He repeated the remark in Spanish to Alma.

Alma nodded. We said, "Gracias."

Inside Danny's room we sat on the bed.

"You look very pretty," I said.

"Thank you. And how is the pain in your chest?"

"Much better," I said. This wasn't strictly true. I put my hand on her wrist. "You are a very good nurse."

We had met at a hospital. I was a soldier, an American in a foreign land. Alma was a nurse. Hemingway and Von Konsky, déjà vu all over again. Instead of going back to war, I went to jail.

Kissing, embracing, one thing led to another. I forgot I was in prison. If I'd had a choice between escaping and staying with Alma . . . I didn't know what I'd do. Clearly, I wasn't thinking straight.

A knock on the door announced visiting hours were over. Alma and I put Danny's bed back together. We walked to the entrance and said, "Hasta luego," until later. Everybody in the tank was in a good mood on visiting day. Proof that conjugal visits improve morale.

The excitement of seeing Alma was too much for me in my weakened condition. Next day, I was sicker. Fever, chills, lightheadedness, coughing. Cigarettes didn't seem to help. I'd broken my promise to God that I'd quit if He got me out of the prison hospital. Now I'd be going back for another fresh air cure.

36

We parked by the hospital, but instead of going around back to the prison ward, we went inside the main building. I was taken to a room on the second floor, at the end of the hall. In the room a real hospital bed had sheets, a blanket, and a pillow. There was a table, two chairs, and glass in the window. Also, a bathroom with a shower. In one of the chairs sat a policeman.

My parents had arranged through their Mexican attorney to have me admitted to the regular hospital. They were paying for a private room with a guard on duty twenty-four hours a day. I wondered what it cost. My parents would spend every dime to help me. Economically, I needed to recover quickly.

A nurse with a clipboard arrived; we filled out some forms. The nurses dressed like nuns. Maybe they were nuns. Mostly they were very professional. A few seemed over the hill, pensioners on assignment where they couldn't screw anything up.

Next morning, I was taken somewhere in the hospital for a test. A tiny ancient nun carried my IV bottle as we pattered down the corridor, followed by a guard. The old nun stared at the floor and mumbled. I don't think she was praying, but practicing her resignation speech:

> Sure and I'd rather take soup from the Protestants . . . I've emptied
> lepers' bedpans in moth eaten jungles . . . prayerfully averted my
> gaze from naked savages fornicating at the drop of a hat . . . and this
> is how I spend my golden years—lugging bottles of who knows
> what for cheap thugs . . . sure and it's a fine thing.

I couldn't understand a word she said. But her miserable expression, when she looked up to keep from walking into a wall, conveyed sour grapes. I've seen prayerful countenances; this old nun didn't look like a happy camper.

As we moved down the hall, she'd stagger off to one side or the other. The plasma bottle she carried, attached to an IV tube, jerked at my wrist. I'd look over to see which way to go. The bottle of clear fluid was filling with blood. From the bottle to my wrist the plastic tube was red. She held the container waist-high, like a lunch pail of burgoo sandwiches for her father in the coal mine. Her waist was two feet above the floor; my wrist, three feet. We had a gravitational imbalance.

I considered tapping her on the shoulder, but she didn't seem to have any shoulders. Startled from her reverie, she might drop the IV bottle and send billowing waves of my blood coursing down the halls. Carefully, I waved my non-IV-attached hand under her nose. She looked up. I pointed to the red bottle. Annoyed, she raised the jug a foot or so, reversing the process. Mumbling, she returned to scrutinizing the linoleum, while I watched the bottle.

We completed our journey and got back to my hospital room. The guard was huffing and puffing. He explained he was suffering from pleurisy, a lung disease worse than pneumonia. Often in the past, he'd coughed up blood. We agreed he was much sicker than I was. As a young man, the guard worked for many years in the Salinas Valley of California, traveling north as far as Ukiah. Missing his family, he returned to Mexico. Now in his forties, he was a policeman. The job paid very little.

The next day was my birthday, May 14th, a Saturday. My parents came to visit. The guard left the room and sat in the hall. I think he was supposed to be stationed there anyway, but when no one was around he'd come in and visit.

My father said the U.S. Army was working through official channels. Our congressman was concerned. He was doing everything possible, but these things take time. Our American lawyer in Calexico said we'd hit a snag. The Mexican attorney had tried to bribe the wrong person in Tijuana. That way was stalled until the damage could be undone. The right person needed to be bribed in order to correct the injudicious bribe.

The American lawyer told my father, in strictest confidence, that in his opinion it wasn't so much the wrong person who'd been bribed, but the wrong amount. Feathers were ruffled, said the attorney, but the dust would settle. My father told me these things as though a breakthrough could occur at any moment and I'd be released. I could see he didn't believe it, though.

While my parents and I visited, a staff lady parked her cart in the doorway. She unloaded a tray and set supper on my side table. On a plate with pink rice and peas were several small animal parts. Limbs hacked off a guinea pig, maybe.

"What's that on your plate?" asked my father.

"I don't know," I said, "I'll ask her. Que es eso?"

"Que?" she asked.

I pointed to the animal appendages. "Eso."

"Ah," she said, "ranas."

"They're ranas," I told my father.

"What the hell are ranas?" he asked.

"Como se dice," I said to the lady, "ranas en Anglice?"

She thought for a moment and in a deeper voice said, "Re-deep, re-deep."

My mom smiled but my father didn't see the humor. He wondered why you'd feed frog legs to some one suffering from malnutrition.

I ate a spoonful of rice to keep my strength up. The milk tasted awful, but I drank half a glass. The staff lady returned and loaded my tray of untouched frog legs onto the cart. She gazed lovingly at the appendages. It seemed unnecessary to ask if she wanted them. They may have lived in her garden.

Leaving the room, she smiled and said, "Re-deep."

Mom and I laughed. My father almost smiled as he walked to the one window in the room that overlooked a busy street. He watched the traffic. The window didn't open. It was divided into small glass panes leaded into sections of a large iron frame.

I had given some thought to the window. Even if I broke a pane, I couldn't fit through the opening. I'd have to break four panes, then hacksaw through four steel frames, each an inch thick. When I climbed through the hole, I'd be dropping from the second story onto a busy sidewalk in the heart of town. If the guard in the hall didn't hear me hacksawing, people in the street would see me taking the window apart.

We were listening to a Dodgers game from Chavez Ravine on a portable radio my parents brought. The guard outside was leaning back in his chair, talking with one of the staff ladies. I could hear his chair tap against the wall.

My father went in the bathroom. When he returned, he sat in a chair next to my bed and glanced at the open doorway. The Dodgers had rallied, scoring a couple of runs. The crowd was noisy. In a low voice, my father asked if I could climb through the bathroom window.

I went into the bathroom and looked at the window again. It was about twelve inches wide, two feet high, and three feet off the floor. The window consisted of a series of ten or so thick glass louvers. Each was fastened on both ends by metal brackets crimped at the corners. Outside the window, mounted against the wall, was a heavy insect screen. The louvers could be cranked open until they hit the screen.

Back in the room, I sat on the bed. My father was waiting for an answer.

"Sure," I said. "I can do it."

"Good."

My mom sat without saying a word. I wondered if she knew what we were talking about.

"How're you going to get the window apart?" I asked.

Before my father answered, we glanced at the doorway to see if anyone was eavesdropping.

"I'll bring some tools. Tomorrow night."

My mom was silent, but if the plan had been put to a vote, she looked like she'd vote against it.

37

The next night after supper, my father returned alone. He said Ma wasn't feeling well. She'd stayed at the motel. The guard left the room and sat outside in the hall. On the radio the Dodgers game had started. I turned it up a little.

"What'd you have for supper tonight?" my father asked. "Cape buffalo or snails?"

"I couldn't tell. It was chopped up with noodles and a mayonnaise sauce."

"I'm parked one block from the hospital," he said quietly. "Maybe a hundred yards from this room."

Before the visit my father had reconnoitered the area. Standing on the sidewalk, he could see my bathroom window. Outside the window was the roof of a single story room. Adjacent to the room was an alley leading to the main street. All I had to do was walk across the roof, drop down to the alley, and make my way to the sidewalk. My father would drive up and I'd get in the car. I liked the sound of that, so simple.

"Wait on the sidewalk," he said. "Don't go looking around for me. When I see you come out of the alley, I'll turn on my headlights and drive to you."

"Where're the tools?" I asked.

He patted his pockets, but nothing rattled.

I was wearing a hospital gown. My clothes were in the closet. Watching the open doorway, I grabbed my stuff out of the closet and went into the bathroom. I put my clothes between the wall and the toilet. Back in the room I sat on the bed.

My father stood up. "Give me ten minutes to get to the car."

"I'll turn on the shower, get dressed, then go out the window."

"Good." He went in the bathroom and closed the door.

I sat on the bed staring at the doorway. I thought I should pay attention to the game on the radio. What if the guard asked me who was winning? I didn't know the score; I couldn't even remember who the Dodgers were playing. I listened carefully.

The announcers talked about some rookie who had been called up from Albuquerque. The rookie was happy to be in the majors. Life in the minors was tough: riding buses, eating greasy food, changing clothes in cheap, cramped locker rooms. It was a sad story but I had my own problems.

Until now I'd been nervously apprehensive. Now I was scared, shaking in my shower shoes. My heart was pounding. I had pains in my shoulder, nausea, lightheadedness. All the signs of a massive coronary. It felt like a cape buffalo was sitting on my chest.

I wondered if I should warn my father. Stop him before it was too late to put the window back together. Maybe he hadn't started yet. The only noise I heard came from the radio. Suddenly I realized: if they caught my father, they'd throw him in jail, too!

What if a nurse came in and needed to get something from the bathroom? A glass of water, an enema hose, whatever? What if the guard needed to take a leak? I tried to think of how many things could go wrong. Hundreds, thousands.

Maybe we should've discussed the cons of the situation. Possibly, a vote should've been taken. As the swing vote, I can see where I might've gone either way. Thank God, Ma wasn't here. They'd lock her up, too.

Coming out of the bathroom, my father closed the door and glanced around the room. That was too quick. Something must've gone wrong, some unforeseen snag. He probably had to go buy more tools.

"Give me ten minutes to get to the car," he said, almost out of breath.

As he went through the doorway, pliers handles were sticking up from his back pocket. Before I could warn him, he was out of sight. Sweet Jesus!

Without a watch I'd have to guess at the time, or count to six hundred. One thousand one, one thousand two . . . too slow. I turned the ball game a little louder. It was too loud. I turned it down. I wondered how much time had passed.

What was I thinking? It'd take ten minutes just to change clothes. In the bathroom I closed the door and turned on the shower full force. My clothes were by the wall. Also stacked by the wall was a pile of glass louvers. The window was open, glass gone, mesh cut out. He must have tossed the piece of screen onto the roof.

Taking off the hospital gown, I picked up my trousers. I didn't need underwear. Sitting on the toilet, I put on my shoes. I didn't need socks. I put on my shirt. It was time to go.

38

With the light on in the bathroom, I was afraid someone in the street would see me climb out the window. My father had spotted the window from the sidewalk. However, if the guard saw the light off beneath the door and heard the shower running full blast, he might think something peculiar was happening. Should I worry about the captors I'm fleeing, or those I might encounter? I turned the light off.

Climbing on the window sill, I hoisted myself sideways into the opening. Gradually, using my feet as brakes, I lowered myself down the outside wall. My shirt caught on a jagged edge of screen and was pulled up to my head. Releasing my grip on the window frame with one hand, I tore the shirt loose from the screen and dropped onto a tar and gravel roof. Noisy gravel, probably ordered special.

Lights were on in the adjacent room; the next several windows were also lit. All the lights were behind bathroom windows of frosted glass louvers. Walking across the roof, gravel crunched under my shoes. Hopefully, the room below was an office. Everyone would be home at this hour. I tiptoed, but the gravel still crunched. If not an office, I hoped it was the deaf ward.

The far wall went down into a dark alley. I climbed over the edge and dropped, almost landing on a garbage can. Plastic bags and cans were everywhere. The alley was wide enough for a small vehicle. Twenty feet away was the sidewalk. People were walking by.

A couple stopped outside the alley. Maybe they heard me land as I made contact with a garbage can. The man looked like a plain clothes detective; the woman could've been an off-duty meter maid. It was too late to hide behind the can. I walked out of the alley, past the couple on the sidewalk.

"Buenas dias," I said, although it was night.

They didn't answer. They pretended not to hear, but checked my movement with quick, sneaky peeks.

Standing at the curb, I looked up and down the busy street. I must be late, or early. It's amazing how slow time goes by when you're escaping from prison. The couple watched me. I couldn't go back in the alley. They probably figured I was a cat burglar, a second story man with pockets full of heart pacers and enema hoses.

Getting down the wall, I could've used some hoses tied together. Instead of dropping into the alley, I would've lowered myself, bungee-style. A soft, quiet landing.

All the parking spaces along the curb were filled with cars. My father didn't say in which direction he was parked. Maybe he was circling the block. If everybody in these cars was visiting patients, an epidemic must have occurred.

The couple at the alley was gone, probably to find a cop. That's it. When the police come, I'm out of here—left, right, or straight ahead. A light blue, unmarked car double-parked. The driver leaned over and rolled down the passenger window. My father waved at me. I jumped off the curb and into the car.

"Don't stop for anything," I said. I was more nervous than I'd been all night.

"This is a rented car," said my father, calmly, following the flow of traffic. "I'll drive it through a brick wall if I have to." He gripped the steering wheel with both hands. There was no one I'd rather have driving my get-a-way car. We made a left turn onto a main thoroughfare.

The guard probably caught on to the shower ploy and had put out an all-points bulletin. I wondered how many years I could get for attempted escape. And, destruction of property, wasting water, scaring tourists. I'd be charged with whatever happened in town tonight.

I saw some toll booths ahead. "Is that the border?"

"That's it."

"What if they try to stop us?"

"They've been waving me through."

We got to the border; the guards waved us through. We were back in the U.S. of A. I pounded the dashboard and punched the headliner.

"Holy shit, Pa," I yelled. "We did it!" Crossing the border with my father in a rented car was the single most wonderful experience I'd ever had. Pa didn't say anything, but he relaxed. He was driving with one hand on top of the steering wheel, just like old times.

We drove to a room my parents rented in a Calexico motel. Ma was glad to see me, but she still had some doubts about the wisdom of my escape. The other lady in the room was the motel manager. She'd been giving my parents whatever information she could.

"You've got to leave here right away," said the motel lady. "Don't stop until you get to L.A. When they find he's gone, they'll come across the border looking for him. First thing, they check motels. It's illegal, but they'll take him back at gunpoint."

My father got his electric razor from the bathroom and tossed it into a suitcase open on the bed. My mom threw in some things, thanked the motel lady, and we were off for L.A. It was after midnight by the car clock. I sat in the back seat, slouched down in case the Federales were already combing the roads.

A few hours of driving got us into the outskirts of Los Angeles. My father decided we could use some rest, so we checked into a motel for a few hours sleep. During breakfast in the coffee shop, Pa called Major Smith and told him what had happened, where we were. Smith said it would be best to drive to Fort MacArthur in San Pedro and report at the provost marshall's office.

Arriving around noon, we followed signs to the office. My father and I went inside while my mom waited in the car parked under a tree. Behind a tall, judicial-style bench sat a sergeant. His head and the tops of his shoulders were all that were visible. I began explaining what had happened.

"Wait a minute," he said.

I heard him roll paper into a typewriter. He asked my name, service number, company, post . . . on and on. My father sat on a wooden bench against the wall.

Completing the form, the sergeant said, "Come with me."

We went through a door behind the desk into a room with three cells, all empty. The sergeant directed me inside the first cell and locked the iron gate. My father pointed out that I had arrived of my own free will. It was no use.

"Standard procedure," said the sergeant.

"I'll be right back," said my father. "I'm going to call Major Smith."

The sergeant closed the door to the cell room. It was the first time I'd been alone since guard duty in the desert. I didn't have to worry about someone sneaking up on me. The silence was eerie. The cell spotless. I thought of all the places I should've gone instead of here.

Paris, France—where the notorious draft-dodger Sylvester Stallone was hiding.

Oxford, England—where the poor draft-dodger William Clinton was sharpening his wits.

Closer to home: the backyard tennis court of super patriot, draft-dodger Rush Limbaugh who practiced his game every afternoon on the same knee his family doctor declared unfit for military service.

At Fort Leonard Wood on the wall of the company day room was a large sign. "The Army Takes Care of its Own." Really? I could start making my own signs. I'd begin with, "When Do They Do That?" and "How Do You Define 'Care' and 'Own'?"

Possibly I was wallowing in self-pity, but I was almost enjoying it. The taste of sour grapes is kind of sweet. Actually, I should be on my knees kissing the floor of my cell. For the first time in forty-four days I could sit quietly alone, nutball free.

In less than an hour, I was released from the stockade. My father had called Major Smith; Smith called the sergeant. The sergeant gave me a map of the post. I was told to report to Headquarters Company, high-lighted by an "X" on the map. I'd be temporarily assigned there. It was two buildings away.

Outside the provost marshall's office in the parking lot, my parents and I said good-bye. Tomorrow was a work day; my father had to be back. They'd turn the car in at the airport and catch a flight home.

"We'll get together soon," said my mom.

"Maybe I'll get a pass and come home." I had a better chance of being elected Pope.

"Good-bye, son," said my father. "Take care."

"I will. Thanks, Dad. Via con Dios."

As they drove away, my mom was visible through the rear window, waving. I kept waving even after the car had turned the corner and they were no longer in sight.

POSTAMBLE

When I got back to Fort Leonard Wood, Missouri, I was court-martialed and convicted of being absent without leave. I pleaded guilty to the charges at the advice of my court appointed lieutenant. His advice was: "If you know what's good for you . . ." My sentence was "to forfeit $20.00 per month for one month, to be confined at hard labor for one month, to be reduced to the grade of Private E-1." Next day, Lt. Colonel Asmus, the commanding officer, suspended the portion adjudging confinement at hard labor for one month.

I wasn't AWOL when I left the desert camp; I had a weekend pass. But, I exceeded the mileage limitation by twenty-two miles.

Brian wasn't court-martialed for his misadventure in Mexico. He was no longer in my battalion. One day I saw him sitting alone in the PX drinking coffee. He recognized me walking toward him. As I reached his table, he said, "Hey, when did they let you out?"

"Not soon enough," I answered. "How come they let you go?"

"I don't know. They called me in and said, 'Leave.'"

"You owe me ten bucks," I said.

"Why's that?"

"I loaned you money to change tanks, remember?"

"That's right. But it's not collectible."

"How come?"

"Because loans made in a foreign country aren't collectible in the United States."

I put my glasses on the table next to Brian's coffee cup. "I'm glad you said that."

"Why?" He stopped grinning.

"Because now I'm going to beat the fuck out of you."

"Hey, can't you take a joke? I was kidding." Brian got his wallet and pulled out a ten-dollar bill. "Here. We're even."

I never saw him again. Months later, a good lieutenant who'd been at my court-martial stopped me outside battalion headquarters.

"Hear about your buddy?" The lieutenant asked.

"Which buddy would that be? I have many, sir."

"Brian what's-his-face. He got a Bad Conduct Discharge."

"What'd he do?"

"He was stealing parachutes and storing them in his wall locker."

"No shit. Really?"

"Really."

I served my two years, plus forty-four days, and received an Honorable Discharge. The urge to re-enlist was compelling, but I resisted.

LAW OFFICES
LEWIS A. PLOURD

Commanding Officer
Fort Leonard Wood
Fort Leonard Wood, Missouri

Dear Sir:

My information is that the above subject is to be court martialed under a special Court on Tuesday, August 11, 1964, under the Code on the charge of absence without leave.

The undersigned represented the subject in coordination with the Legal Officer, Major Dorsey, of Fort MacArthur and also in coordination with legal assistance from the country of Mexico in connection with his absence from his base of operations and his confinement in Mexico.

Based on my experience and knowledge of the facts of the arrest and confinement in question and without reservation on my part, the arrest and confinement was without probable cause as we define it under our standard definitions of jurisprudence in this country.

It would be very much appreciated if a copy of this letter be forwarded to his Unit Commanding Officer and also to Lt. Saccaro whom I understand is Defense Counsel on the case.

Very truly yours,

LEWIS A. PLOURD

```
Mileage Limitations
Retreat to Midnight - 40 miles
24 hr period - 100 miles
36 hr period - 150 miles
48 hr period - 200 miles
72 hr period - 250 miles
```

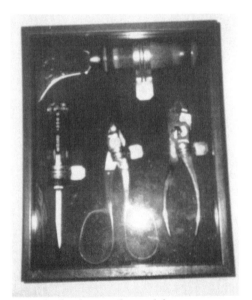

Shadowbox tools used for escape

Bibliography

Abbey, Edward, *The Serpents of Paradise*. Henry Holt and Company., New York, 1996

Darlington, David, *The Mohave*. Henry Holt & Co., New York, 1996

Traven, B., *March to the Monteria*. Hill and Wang, New York, 1971

Trimbell, Marshall, *Roadside History of Arizona*. Mountain Press Publishing Co., Missoula, Montana, 1986

LEWIS HORTON was born in Detroit, Michigan. After serving in the United States Army (Honorable Discharge), he worked as a truck driver, ironworker, real estate agent, property manager, and oyster pirate in San Pablo Bay. His next book, *Everything Is With You Always*, is in the works.